The Man 'Who
Said 'No' To The
THE BEATLES

Pete "Jam side down" Maclaine

EMPIRE
PUBLICATIONS
MANCHESTER

First published in 2011.

EMPIRE PUBLICATIONS
1 Newton Street, Manchester M1 1HW
© Pete Maclaine 2011

ISBN 1 901 746 76 3 - 9781901746761

Cover design & layout: Mathew Faulkner
Cover photograph of me and Paul: © My cousin Alan Pearce -1963

A great big thank you to my friend Mathew for his patience and hard work designing the book for me.

Disclaimer:

In writing this book I have tried my best to get the details right. I am hoping my memory has served me well... Pete.

Printed in Great Britain.

For my children Simon, Louise and Nicholas, who still give me butterflies.

For my grandchildren Eve and Delius.

For the Clan, Graham Attwood, Dave Barrow and Steve Gibson. The Hottest Rock 'n' Roll band around. For keeping me young and letting me sing with them. Thanks.

For my lady Helen, who has had a very difficult and sad three years, but who is always ready to help me with a smile...

My very best friend

I miss you now,
I will miss you again,
I always miss,
My very best friend.

On my return,
I will make amends,
I'll stay close to you,
My very best friend.

But when I'm away,
My thought I will send,
Because I love you,
My very best friend.

Quotes

"After 50 years in the business, there is one thing that has never changed - Pete's enthusiasm. You can guarantee you will get one hundred and ten percent entertainment value".
Derek Quinn, lead guitar, Freddie and the Dreamers.

"I have been a friend of Pete's for a very long time, this book is a credit to him".
Michael Cohen, The Hollies first manager and owner of The Toggery.

"Very interesting to read, I don't know how he remembers it all".
Dave Barrow, bass player and an authority on Robinson's Mild.

"Pete was Manchester's original number one Rock 'n' Roll star. I saw him for the first time at the Oasis Club, Lloyd St. in 1961, and unlike many of his contemporaries, he's still rockin', still on top form and for me, still Manchester's number one".
Fred Eyre, ex-footballer, author, radio commentator.

"A fine collection of memories, no one better than Pete, who has always been on the scene. A great Mancunian".
Graham "Atty" Attwood, saxophonist.

"Pete is the guardian of Manchester's Rock 'n' Roll fraternity. He also tells great stories".
Kevin Parrott, guitarist and one half of Brian & Michael who had a number one hit with Matchstalk Men.

Pete's poetry has been heard on BBC Radio Manchester, with Fred Fielder and The WOW Show with Jimmy Wagg and Eamon O'Neil.

Contents

Jam Side Down Maclaine

I said Doctor listen to me,
I don't feel too well,
I've gone and lost the woman I love,
And you're the only one I can tell,
Put your head close to my heart,
Give it a bang, get my pulse to start,
Hey Doc' now I feel okay,
Just give me some pills, I'll be on my way.

I said barman listen to me,
I know you listen good,
I know you've heard it all before,
But just one more time if you could,
Fill my glass right to the top,
I'll keep drinking, I'll tell you when to stop,
Hey, barman now I feel alright,
Just get me a taxi, and I'll say goodnight.

I said lady listen to me,
I know you'll understand,
So, I've had a little drink or two,
But I'm still a man,
I don't mind if I have to pay,
Lie me down I'll do anything you say,
Hey, what I got you can keep,
But right now I got to get some sleep.

I said officer listen to me,
I know I must look a mess,
How I got into this alley, well,
You can probably guess,
I want to tell you It's been one hell of a night,
Arrest me now, I know you've got the right,
All I want is just one small loan,
Show me the bus stop and I'll go home.

I said Judge listen to me,
You know I'm not a bad man,
Now you've heard my circumstances,
Forgive me if you can,
When I walk out you won't see me again,
I'll forget that woman, I think I can,
Maybe it's best if I leave town,
That way I won't see her around.

I said Warden listen to me,
I know you've got some time,
I'm only locked in this jail of yours,
Because I couldn't pay the fine,
I'm spending one year in prison,
The jury said it was a sin,
But if that women comes knocking on your front door,
Just tell her that I ain't in.

I walk into a bar and it's always the same,
People turn around say, "here he comes again",
Jam Side Down Maclaine.

Manchester

It's expanding heart,
It's changing face,
In all the world,
My favourite place.

Streets full of treasure,
In memories they hold,
Buildings with passion,
Both new and old.

Where I was born,
Always proud to say,
It welcomes me back,
When I've been away.

What was brown,
Is now gold,
This good old town,
Will always be home.

M'Mam, Alice Wetton

She loved to dance, she loved to sing,
She liked a little drink or two,
She gave birth to me on June 30th,
It was 1942.

I was told it was a dark and scary night,
The Luftwaffe high above my protruding head,
Ignoring the hospital I was being born in,
Bombs destined for Trafford Park instead.

Mam lost a child about a year before,
He would have been my brother John,
Not deterred by that devastating loss,
I suppose they just carried on.

Getting married in 1939,
Horrible war had just begun,
Mam making bullets at Mather & Platt.
Longing for a son.

Long working days and blackout nights,
Mancunians fought off depression,
There I was being born like I told you,
Peter Edwin Wetton.

Because of my Dad's engineering skills,
He didn't go off to war,
Mam and me thank God for that,
I might not have been born at all.

Music

We got together in '58,
A pure love affair,
I was young, you were older,
I didn't really care.

You gave me all those words,
Spinning round in my head,
You even made me dress different,
Not caring what people said,

We have been inseparable,
For many, many years,
We've been through so much,
Laughter, and tears.

You were always there,
When ever I was in pain,
I know without you,
Life would not be the same.

I can't remember our anniversary,
I think it was a Thursday night,
When the band playing had no singer,
I was "pushed" to answer their plight,

Up the steps to the youth club stage,
Feeling anything but cool,
Those three minutes would change my life,
I sang Ricky Nelson's, Poor Little Fool.

I wanted to be like Elvis,
I practised all the moves,
Now I'm a singer in a band,
Even bought a pair of Blue Suede Shoes.

Yes, we are still together,
We've had our ups and downs,
On the path that I chose,
Feet firmly on the ground.

The Drovers at the Bodega, 1960

The Dakotas evolved from this line up. Tommy and Pete left and in
came Robin McDonald on rhythm guitar and Ian Fraser on bass. There
was a bass player after Ian but I can't remember his name. He had a
beard and was a good singer! Then eventually, Tony Bookbinder took
over on drums and Ray Jones on bass. The last change as far as me and
the Dakotas was Mike Maxfield replacing Bryn on lead guitar.

Note on guitars below: A Futurerama, Tommy still has it. Two cherry-
red, Les Paul Juniors, classy for the time. I think Bryn had the first
Fender Stratocaster in Manchester, although there are others who claim
this, including Pete Bocking and Bob Gill. This was a great time for
guitarists.

L to R: Tommy Gannon, Me, Pete Walker, Trevor Ebber and Bryn Jones.

My 21st

Belle Vue, June 30th 1963.

Jimmy Saville at the Top Ten Club every Sunday night, the Elizabeth Ballroom. Guest bands each week, Rolling Stones, Manfred Mann, the Springfields. This night it was Sounds Incorporated, they had a hit with Spanish Harlem. They were also Gene Vincent's backing band in England. About 3,000 people every week.

Johnny Hynes, drums, Brian Day, bass, Pete Bocking, guitar. A great night and then back to my parents house, it was aunt and uncle night. The night before, we played the Oasis, that was the party for my friends. Another great night.

Yes I Do / US Mail was released july 1963, it sold out in one day. Unfortunately, the Decca record pressing plant was on holiday so no more records could be pressed. It didn't make the charts. Other recordings didn't escape.

Changing Earth

The earth is rebelling, seems like she had enough,
The abuse she has taken, is anything that tough?
Trees that give life are disappearing,
Man's greed has seen to that.
Is it all too far gone now?
Is there no way back?
Hurricanes becoming more frequent,
With power high on the scale,
It's evil eye on destruction,
And leaving the saddest trail.
Drought in Brazilian rain forest,
The worst for forty years,
Brought on by mankind,
Confirming our deepest fears.
Fires for no apparent reason,
The sun is getting too hot,
The protective shield around us,
Have we all forgot,
The words of eminent scientists,
"Be careful with use of fuels
The ozone layer won't stand it."
But some don't play by the rules.
Inside the earth is erupting,
Not happy with the situation above,
Mankind is intent on destroying,
The planet that some of us love.
Earthquakes of devastating proportion,
With no regard for the rich or the poor,
"Act now" we've been saying for decades,
Or Mother Earth will be no more!

At The Club

Over the years I have compered at quite a few Clubs.

1975, The Broadway Club, Failsworth, Manchester. The Three Degrees played for four nights. Their MD was billed as Sir Richard Barrett. He was a tough, hard case, a bully really and he carried a gun. The sound guy at the club couldn't get it right so Sir Richard brought in someone else and at show time he had our man locked in a room.

I took Sir Richard into Manchester one day, showed him around and had a couple of drinks. It turns out that he was in fact Ritchey Barrett, who recorded "Some Other Guy" on the Motown Records label, the song the Beatles and every beat group in the country, me included, did in 1962. He didn't know, we got on quite well after that.

Manchester City Social Club 1994. I introduce Bernard Manning and then sit down to watch him. He turns to the musicians Tony Baker and Pete Hilton (both in The Dakotas now - funny old world) and says "you bastards have been here for ages", I shout out "not as long as your pianist Dave Green has been at the Embassy Club". Bernard says "he's been with me for 30 years. He thinks he's got the job but I've got two others to try yet". Priceless.

Smithfield Market

Greengrocers fishmongers and florists,
They would come from miles around,
Into the city centre,
To buy the freshest goods in town.

Lorries would travel through the night,
For business to start about five,
The wholesale stalls would be ready,
The market was magic, buzzin', alive.

I worked for Cocozza Wood, on Oak Street,
Managed by my Father-in-law,
One of the most respected men in the market,
His name was "Big Harry" Downward.

The retailers would bid and barter,
To get the best for their little shops,
Lads like me would barrow it to their vans,
For half-crown or a couple of bob.

Trade finished about one or two PM,
We would always go for a pint,
Then a weary ride home on the bus,
You can bet we slept that night.

Now it's the Northern Quarter,
Smithfield Market all gone,
I drink there sometimes in the fashionable bars,
But the memory lingers on.

The facia of the fish hall still standing,
This piece of architecture tells a story,
But I wonder if people in the surrounding apartments,
Really know of it's former glory.

When I was about 9 years old, I would get the bus to Stevenson Sq. Then walk down
Thomas St. past the market to Victoria Station and get the electric train to my Aunty
Emma's house in Radcliffe.

Tommy Duck's

Tommy Duck's was a great Manchester pub,
Full of interest and diversity,
With ladies knickers pinned to the ceiling,
And none of them were dirty.

It was surrounded by terraced houses,
But that was a long time ago,
At the end it stuck out in a car park,
But it was still the place to go.

Behind the bar the largest display of whiskeys,
More than any pub in the land,
On some nights while drinking fine ales,
Entertained by a local jazz band.

On the walls there were lots of pictures,
Hollywood and music hall stars,
Fun to see people scratching their heads,
Trying to guess who they are.

The landlord at Tommy's,
Looked a bit like he was dead,
When he left they carried him in a coffin,
All the way round to the Nag's head.

The Bridgewater Hall was coming,
Tommy Duck's was in the way,
It's land was to be redeveloped,
For the brewery, a big payday.

When Saturday night drinkers left the building,
Tommy's doors were closed for good,
The bulldozers flattened it overnight,
Next morning just Manchester mud.

I know you can't stand in the way of progress,
And money with all its might,
But someone could have told me,
I was going to Tommy's that night.

Tommy Duck's - Originally The Princes Tavern, 1867. Named after landlord Tommy
Duckworth. Closed 1991.

Saturday Matinee

Going to the Saturday matinee,
When I was about seven or eight,
Taken by older kids,
All excited, the memories are great.

After a week with just the radio,
Dick Barton, Treasure Island, Journey into Space,
Now going to the pictures,
I couldn't get the smile from my face.

Chewing our Wine Gums,
Waiting for the show to start,
A big cheer when the lights dimmed,
And left us in the dark.

The curtains would go back,
And reveal a giant screen,
With a colourful Warner Brothers sign,
A cartoon we hoped we hadn't seen.

It didn't really matter,
Everybody's a Bugs Bunny fan,
And once again he outwits,
That pesky Yosemite Sam.

Then it was the serial Flash Gordon,
With his rocket ship on strings
Propelled by sparklers,
Back then the most convincing thing.

On his fabulous horse Diablo,
We roared on the Cisco Kid,
Chasing the baddies out of town,
They got booed, they always did.

It's laughter time next,
With Curly, Larry and Mo,
The hilarious Three Stooges,
They always stole the show.

The poking in the eyes,
The slapping on their heads,
The comical, musical snoring,
When asleep in their beds.

A big cheer for Tom and Jerry,
Our favourite cat and mouse,
Chasing a hundred miles an hour,
In the World's longest house.

Amazing how they try to kill each other,
With dynamite and exploding cigars,
It takes Butch the dog to intervene,
To show what friends they really are.

Roy Rogers and Trigger were my favourites,
They always got their man,
They certainly got this one,
Because I am still a fan.

The lights go up, the show is over,
We scramble for the door,
We've only got a week to wait
Then we can all come back for more.

Newton Heath

My Mother's Dad, my Granddad Isaac,
Lived at 14 Thomson Street, Newton Heath,
I remember him quite vividly,
Because he didn't have any teeth.

He would suck on his old brown pipe,
Stuffed with rough shag,
I can smell the tobacco now,
God, it was bad.

They made me smoke it once,
Caught with a cigarette, about thirteen,
I remember the room spinning round,
Then turning a sickly shade of green.

My "real" Grandma had died some years before,
"Old Ike" had married again,
A Yorkshire lass called Mary,
She was my Nana and my friend.

When ever I had to be minded,
It was Nana Mary who looked after me,
From an old rockin' chair she sang me songs,
I must have been about three.

My Mam and Dad would drop me off,
We didn't live too far away,
In a small rented semi,
171 Monsal Road, Harpurhey.

After a couple of hours out, they'd pick me up,
Into my trolley, and head back to 171,
Once there, my Dad would go in first,
To make sure all the cockroaches had gone.

Old Ike

Old Ike worked for Kerr and Ogger,
It was a cotton dyers mill,
But for the humidifier,
It might have been there still.

The "knocker up" would wake him,
Then he'd walk down the canal path,
Mam would take me there some evenings,
So I could have a bath.*

At night Old Ike would go for a pint,
To the Greyhound Inn at the end of the street,
Play darts on a Manchester "log end",
He was the man to beat.

When my grandad fancied a drink in the house,
He would send me across the street,
To Jewsburys the outdoor beer license,
He didn't know, but it really was a treat.

A white jug full of Wilsons mild and bitter,
With a lovely creamy top.
I would stop when half way back,
And sip the beer through the froth.

* I'd have a bath in a big tub that was used to dye the cotton. A log end was a dartboard about 2 inches thick. No trebles, the doubles about 3mm and a small 50 bull. Songs we sang - Ragtime Cowboy Jo, She'll Be Coming Round the Mountain.

Isaac's "Kids"

My mother Alice had a sister, Emma,
A smart brother called Sam,
Then the family favourite Eric,
He was the youngest of this clan,

My Dad Ted married my mother,
Sam married my Dad's sister, Ada,
It looks straightforward written here,
But it got quite confusing later.

Sunday School

Apparently, the first time I went to Sunday school,
I came home with a worried look,
When asked about my disgruntled face, I said.
I'm not going next week, Jesus didn't turn up.

Belle Vue - Funground of the North

My Dad would say, it's a lovely day,
What can we do?
He always did this when he had something up his sleeve,
In fact he already knew.

Lets get ready, we'll have a day out,
I'll take you to Belle Vue Zoo,
Then off we'd go to catch the bus,
The 98 or 82.

Starting to get excited now,
Still no sign of rain,
Not far down Oldham Road,
Just to Hulme Hall Lane.

Then jump on the 53,
That would take us all the way,
Across Hyde Road, through the turnstile,
Where we all had to pay.

We were really there now,
It's confirmed by the smell,
The fish and chips, the elephant house,
I remember oh so well.

Belle vue was established by John Jennison in 1825.

Belle Vue 2 - The Bobs

Walking past the watershute,
People pay to get wet through,
I suppose like me, being Mancunians,
It is something that they're used to.

You could wobble on the hump of a camel,
Watch chimpanzees have their tea,
Ride high on an Indian elephant,
As a kid, not much fun for me.

For me it was the Bobs*,
A magical roller coaster ride,
This giant fairground attraction,
Gave me butterflies inside.

Once in your seat you start the journey,
To the sky, then thundering down,
Twisting and turning at 90 miles an hour,
All this for half a crown.

*Opened 1929

Painting by Stuart Johnson

All the rides were great,
The Waltzer, the Ghost Train for secret hugs,
Even the Scenic Railway,
When you couldn't afford the Bobs.

Just walking round the Zoological gardens,
Seeing animals and birds up close,
Hardly any television sets then,
We were luckier than most.

A few years later as teenagers,
Me and my pals would venture back,
To watch Belle Vue Aces on Saturday night,
Speedway on a dangerous cinder track.

Peter Craven was our hero then,
He seemed to win all the races,
They sing the same chant today,
Give me an A, give me a C, give me an E, give me an S...ACES

The Aces moved down the road,
The animals had to go,
Too late for investment,
It was the end of the show.

The site now all sorts of buildings,
People drive by quite unaware,
But me and thousands of others,
Wishing it was still there.

Cricket M'Dad and me...

My Dad taught me to bowl,
when I was just a lad,
I really loved the game
and got quite cricket mad.

He spent time, taught me well,
I captained my school team,
To carry on and play for Lancashire,
That, was my dream.

Early 50's we'd go to Old Trafford,
To watch Washbrook and Statham play,
I loved being there with him,
Egg and tomato butties made my day.

For long and peaceful days,
We both enjoyed the game,
I never really got bored,
And I can't remember rain.

Dad died in 2000,
But I still talk to his cap,
It's hanging in the hallway,
Some people think I'm mad.

I don't care what people say,
I like our little chat,
You never know one day,
It might even talk back!

Simon got a hatrick and the winning runs,
with his Son, Dad and Grandad there.

Market Street

Market Street starts at Piccadilly,
At Lewis's where the arcade used to be,
At night ladies of ill repute,
But always Wyles Toy Shop to me.

Models of ships and aeroplanes,
Dinky toys, some of which I had,
Fabulous boxes of Meccano,
I made all sorts of things with my Dad.

Across the street the Ryland's building,
Then Pauldens and now Debenhams,
The Street now pedestrianised,
But watch out for those electric trams.

The old Market Street had cars and buses,
The infamous Listons Bar,
The U.C.P. half way down,
Not too far from the Fatted Calf.

Just off the Street at the bottom,
Once stood the Thatched House pub,
A watering hole for printers then,
When Manchester was a newspaper hub.

Market Street now, in this modern city,
Different cultures, every kind,
The atmosphere heightened by buskers,
And a smile never hard to find.

Old Harold

When Old Harold died,
He had lived just down the street,
It was quite expected,
He was ninety three.

A fine old chap,
Who had lived through wars,
Always dressed very smart,
An example to us all.

To have him cremated,
Was his family's plea,
But Harold's old Navy friends,
Wanted him buried at sea.

They all sat and wondered,
Who was going to win,
They decided to compromise,
So they poached him.

Beatles at the Oasis

It was Friday February 2nd 1962 when the Beatles first came to
Manchester to play at the Oasis Club, Lloyd St. They were booked by
Rik Dixon, who was the manager and agent of me and the Dakotas. Of
course the Oasis was our home, we were there every Tuesday night, and
most Sundays. It was ironic that on that very same Friday night, Rik
had booked us to play at the Cavern in Liverpool for the first time. We
shared the bill with the Red River Jazzmen. The Beatles were in our
house and we were in theirs. We were the first Manchester group to
play the Cavern at the beginning of the beat era.

At that time the beat boom was just getting underway and not many
people in Manchester had heard of the fab four. Friday was always busy,
that night there were only 37 people who paid to see the band. I will
never understand it. Next time they played there, the place was packed
and the queue was up Lloyd Street into Albert Square. I was there that
night, they were fabulous. When they finished I took them to a party.
I had arranged it earlier, drinks and girls. It was at a friends house
whose parents were on holiday. Mostly it was good clean fun, they were
always very funny, although there was a little hanky panky behind closed
bedroom doors. I remember sharing "Purple Hearts" with John Lennon.

I took them out a few times when they were in Manchester. I
remember one time we were all in our van. When Paul asked me "Do
you mind if we do A Taste Of Honey". The groups in those days played
songs from the Hit Parade and Rock 'n' Roll. I like to think I was a little
bit different because I sang a few swingers a la Bobby Darin, Mack the
knife, Beyond the sea, Stepping Out With My Baby etc. The Beatles of
course changed everything.

Pete Best

Manchester 1961 (Oasis and Club Roma)

You must have been about seventeen,
When I caught your eye in that dark coffee bar,
It was underground, you could not see the light of day.

We had frothy coffee and a Coca Cola,
I had to kiss you before I got much older,
I could not resist those lips.

We had twist, and then a smooch,
You got makeup on my mohair suit,
I didn't mind, I had another one at home.

Over in a corner Alan Clarke and Graham Nash
Two ambitious Salford lads,
Who were destined for fortune and fame

Freddy was a dreamer, Wayne Fontana still a kid
I knew they both would make it,
And that's exactly what they did.

When we had to get out of there,
So climbing up the stairs
Into a city that was inviting us to play.

Round the corner, not too far,
Walking to my favourite bar,
Where the band played on into the night.

I asked if you'd like a bowl of soup,
I can see you've been working out with a hula-hoop,
You said no but I'll have a Cherry B.

I had my usual bottle of beer,
And a whisky mac to keep my head clear,
Back then that's what did it for me,

In a candle lit room we had fillet steak and chips,
I could well afford the twelve and six,
Man we were cool.

It was quite late when you phoned your mother,
Saying not to worry, but,
You would not be home that night.

Manchester 1961,
Manchester, we had a whole lot of fun,
Manchester 1961.

And the Beatles yet to come!!!

Club Roma was owned by champion wrestler Tommy Mann and is still
trading today on Bloom Street.

Beatles at the Cavern

We'd played in Liverpool a few times,
At the Cavern, and various places,
We knew of the Beatles and their names,
But we had never seen their faces.

Gerry and the Pacemakers, we had worked with,
The Mersey Beats and the fabulous Big Three,
But, the group all the fuss was about,
We still had yet to see.

One night, Mr Epstein came to see us,
We told him of our plight,
He said he would do his best,
And get us a gig together one night.

He was a man of his word,
The lovely Mr Epstein,
Not night, a lunchtime session at the Cavern,
It was the fullest we've ever seen.

We setup and went on first,
I can still feel the thrill,
The crowd were having fun and clapping,
But really waiting for the top of the bill.

The Dakotas

I must admit for a group from Manchester,
We went down very well,
Then into the dressing room at the side of the stage,
For an experience I've been longing to tell.

I sat in a corner, in my sweat stained suit,
Adrenaline still running through my veins,
I didn't know then, but from that moment on,
Things would never be the same.

"They" came in the room like they lived there,
I suppose it was really their home,
Like aliens coming back to their mother ship,
Nobody was going to steal their throne.

I viewed this from under my towel,
I could feel the room was changing,
The Cavern was eighteen stone steps down,
But it felt like it was elevating.

Me and Paul McCartney back stage at the Odeon, early 1963

Beatles at the Cavern Cont.

I stood up to greet them,
They introduced themselves one by one,
"Hello I'm John Lennon" in a thick scouse accent,
Like some kind of prodigal son.

Paul McCartney came over, held out his hand,
I shook it and said hello,
I can't really explain what came over me,
But I found it hard letting go.

The room now hot and crowded,
When someone younger looking in comparison,
With a lilting kind of musical voice,
Said "Hi, I'm George Harrison".

Mysterious and not saying much to anyone,
Quite different from the rest,
When he finally came over to me,
Just nodded and said "Pete Best".

We left our new friends to get ready,
To the snack bar, I had a cup of tea,
And when Bob Wooller introduced "The Beatles",
The adoration was plain to see.

Lennon and McCartney were like a rose, McCartney the flower, Lennon the thorns.

THE

DAKOTAS

WITH

PETE MACLAINE

THE DIXON AGENCY,
45 LLOYD STREET,
MANCHESTER, 2.
BLA 6363

Beatles at the Cavern Cont.

The cave dwellers as the Cavern DJ called them,
All excited, and screaming for the band,
But Lennon, with a verse of Onward Christian Soldiers,
Soon had them eating out of his hand.

George Harrison just to the left,
Quite shy, with his quirky smile,
Excellent on his Gretch guitar,
In that rockin' country style.

We'd not seen anything like John Lennon,
Chewing gum and that aggressive stance,
Singing like there was no tomorrow,
He wouldn't give failure a second glance.

Pete Best unperturbed on his drums,
Looking moody and mean,
With his Tony Curtis style hair,
It was he who got most of their screams.

Paul McCartney with a touch of arrogance,
Hidden just behind his boyish face,
Up to the mic' "Long Tall Sally" in G,
Blew us right out of the place.

There we were in a cellar in Liverpool,
Watching a monster of a band,
Not from Baron Frankenstein,
Elvis, Buddy and Chuck they all lent a hand.

We didn't know then, how far they would go,
And influence the world, in more ways than one,
We stand here today, we've all been affected,
And it still goes on, and on, and on.

THIS COMING
FRIDAY
LUNCHTIME

Special Double Bill
ON STAGE

12·20 pm
THE BEATLES

1·00 pm
PETE MACLAINE
& THE DAKOTAS

1·40 pm
THE BEATLES

→ Come Along Early !

Eppy's Birthday

We were playing at the Cavern,
September, 1962,
We'd been in Liverpool all day,
A lunchtime session too.

Just sitting in the dressing room,
Paul McCartney came in to say hello,
He said it was Brian's birthday,
And could I mention it in the show.

I made up some words to the tune of Mr Postman,
I sang them on the mic',
Eppy thought it was very funny,
It was a really good night.

Mr Epstein came to see me,
He said he liked the suit I was wearing,
And could I get him the same material,
To have made up for that special evening.

With my tongue in my cheek,
Doing my best not laugh,
Told him it was African wild silk,
And that I had bought the last.

In fact my stage suits were curtain material,
To confess to that would have been hard,
Bought from a shop in Manchester,
It was only ten bob a yard.

MR EPSTEIN PLEASE TELL ME.
WHEN THE Bs. ARE ON TV.

MR EPSTEIN LOOK AND SEE
HAVE YOU A PHOTO OF THE BIG 3.

GERRY AND THE PACEMAKERS.
THEY ARE GREAT __
WHEN THEYRE ON THE CAVERN DONT BE LATE

~~JON~~ JOHN PAUL GEORGE AND RINGO TOO
WE THINK THEYRE BEST AND WE KNOW YOU DO
NOW WEVE ~~SUNG~~ SUNG OUR LITTLE SONG
                                    FOR YOU
AND WE HOPE YOUR NOT GONNA BOO.

              AW_ NIEMS

      SONG FOR BRIAN EPSTEINS BIRTHDAY.
      SUNG ON THE CAVERN STAGE
                  (ORBEND '62) ~~BEGING~~ (BEGINING)

              SEPT 19 (1934)

Thoughts, after Eppy's Birthday

This is all very well,
Was Eppy my friend, or my foe,
To tell you the truth,
I didn't really know.

Was he there that night,
With an ulterior motive,
Was I so naïve,
That I didn't really notice.

Was he checkin' out my band,
To back his new singer,
When three scouse groups,
Had already give him the finger.

Maybe he didn't recognise my talent,
Or think I was able,
This cheeky young Mancunian,
To fit into his stable.

A few months later,
I knew it couldn't last,
Eppy dangled a carrot,
The band could not pass.

He said "if you back my new protégé,
You get your own record deal",
That's all they ever wanted,
You can almost here the squeal.

To tell you the truth,
They never thought we were equals,
It had never been the same,
Since the day we met the Beatles.

It's all water under the bridge,
I don't hold any grudges,
I am what I am,
And I stand up to my judges.

P.S. Eppy did offer me another group,
A little respect was shown,
And John and Paul would write me a song,
I said "it's ok boys, I'll write my own"... Aaaaaaaaarh.

The Oasis

The Oasis club, Lloyd Street,
Just off Albert Square,
The hottest place in town,
You just had to be there.

Once called the "Two J's"
But Jack Jackson saw the light,
Trad' Jazz fading fast,
So it changed almost over night.

Hugh Goodwin the new owner
The first manager, was Rik Dixon,
Followed by Pauline and Graham Clegg,
Tony Stewart, all in the same direction.

Rosemary Eccles served in the snack bar,
She later became Mrs Nash,
Alan Clark married his girl friend Jennifer,
The record was a smash.

The Bob Gillespie Trio played some lunch times,
Modern jazz in the middle of the day,
At night at Jerry Harris's Piccadilly Club,
Backing top class cabaret.

DJ's MacMagonegall Lacy
I still see him today,
Dave Lee Travis, the hairy monster,
'Till radio fame took him away.

Tuesday nights me with the Dakotas,
Great nights, we had lots of fun,
We even had guests from Liverpool,
"The Four Most" the favourite one.

Sunday was "Star" night,
Some from the USA,
Great to see them right up close,
You know now it's the only way.

Gene Vincent, Bee Bumble and the Stingers,
Tony Orlando from Dawn,
Bruce "Hey Baby" Chanel with Delbert McClinton,
The list goes on and on.

Joe Brown and his Bruvvers, Johnny Kidd and the Pirates,
Larry Parnes "Rockers" came to town,
Bert Weedon with his hit "Guitar Boogie"
Even Rolf Harris tied his "Kangaroo" down.

The Hollies, Herman's Hermits, Wayne Fontana,
All had the biggest say,
Freddie & the Dreamer's, a thousand other groups,
The Oasis paved the way.

L to R: Alan Clark, singer with The Hollies, Pete Maclaine, Graham Nash

The 3 Coins

There is no fountain on Fountain Street,
Only the fountain of youth,
A little place called the 3 Coins,
It was almost concealed from view.

Some nights Jimmy Saville was the DJ,
Spinning the hit parade of the day,
Happy dancing people,
Twisting the night away.

Fashion clad teenagers,
Drinking fizzy stuff and Coke,
No pills, no alcohol being served,
Todays youth would think it a joke.

The 3 Coins also had live music,
Groups heading for the charts,
It was great to see them up close,
Even the Beatles played their part.

Later, no drunks or broken bottles,
Home on the bus, no violence or threat,
Nowadays some idiot might stab you,
Maybe just for a bet.

Fountain Street still there of course,
A new building where the club used to be,
Walking past when in the city,
Happy memories come flooding back to me.

The Beatles played the 3 Coins on 19th November 1961. My good friend Michal Cohen
went there that night to measure them up for leather jackets. Michael owned the Toggery
in Stockport. He was also the "Epstein" to the Hollie's and the Toggery Five. Graham and
myself worked at the shop. In 1962 me and the Dakotas opened the extension, we played
upstairs. All the local groups shopped there.

The night Scotty Moore came to town

He created the riff that became Rock 'n' Roll
That's Alright Mama, it was nineteen fifty four,
In the Sun studios, Memphis Tennessee,
First time I heard it, etched in my memory,

Part of the phenomenon that still exists today,
Truth is, Bill and Scotty didn't get much pay,
Even when Elvis made it, manipulated by Colonel Tom,
The money didn't get much better, sort of dampened the fun.

Although Elvis, Scotty and Bill were great friends,
It was plain to see, the road was coming to an end,
Las Vegas was calling, a new band for certain,
A big one, round a great quartet, featuring James Burton.

Bill Black passed away, Scotty left alone,
After sometime opened a studio, and toured on his own,
I saw him in Manchester some years ago,
Although not too well, it was still a great show.

The night Scotty Moore came to town Cont.

There he was with his Gibson guitar,
All those years, we go back so far,
All us old rockers, but there was no disguise,
Quite a few of us watching with tears in our eyes.

We cheered Scotty off, 'till he got backstage,
Also the Grundy Pritchard band for the show they gave,
We went to the bar, see how drunk we could get,
Mr Moonlight, "Teddy Boy" Lewis, Eric "The Ted",
A nostalgic quartet.

It was one of those nights, you've just got to have,
See someone whose inspired you, with friends, and have a laugh,
This was one to remember, I say with no frown,
That very special night, Scotty Moore came to town.

Sam's Chop House

Situated on the corner,
Of Chapel Walks and Back Pool Fold,
I remember in my younger days,
It always looked very old.

The first time I ventured,
About nineteen sixty three,
Down the winding stairs into Sam's,
A brand new experience for me.

It was the coffee bar era,
The Cona, The Can Can and Mogambo,
Full of young people, mostly girls,
They were the places to go.

It was quite some time later,
When I rediscovered Sam's
Realising it's significance,
Now it's always in my plans.

Bar staff on the ball,
Full of good cheer,
They know now what I drink,
A nice pint of creamy Sam's own beer.

The fabulous restaurant,
The menu Manchester fayre,
Victorian tiled floor, oak panelled walls,
A pleasure, just to be there.

You must visit when in Manchester,
For a drink, or sometimes to dine,
The first time I took Helen, she said,
It's like going back in time.

Psychological Comfort

You can toss and turn all night,
Sleep won't really come,
But when that alarm starts to ring
Turn it off, bleary eyed and glum,
All of a sudden you get that feeling,
That you want to stay in bed,
Snuggle down and get comfy,
Not really caring about the day ahead,
The pillow you've been fighting with,
Is suddenly your best friend,
If only you could stay in bed,
And this feeling never end.

Vasectomy*

They said to me vasectomy,
Two stitches and no pain,
So I had the operation,
Now I don't feel quite the same.

*Sorry, no picture!

Staying Home

You think it's easy, staying home alone,
Doing the garden, answering the phone,
Write down messages, good or bad,
Walk through the hall say hello to my Dad.

Take a trip down to B&Q,
Only on Wednesdays, I get discount too,
Look all around, buy a new paint brush,
I don't mind, it's free on the bus.

I might tidy up, get out the vac',
Disturb the cat, I know she doesn't like that,
I brought in the washing earlier on,
You never know, I might get some ironing done.

I've got the ingredients for the evening meal,
This cooking lark is no big deal,
With a nice glass of Cabernet Sauvignon,
I'm singing and dancing with the radio on.

The table now set for tonights surprise,
I love to see the look in my lady's eyes,
A candlelit dinner, a flower or two,
A nice way of saying I love you.

Food all gone, there is nothing left,
Some people say I could have been a chef,
Got to finish the wine once you start,
We all know it's good for your heart.

Some days are better than others,
Some days don't seem quite so long,
Some days are better than others,
But every day, I sing a song.

My Dad passed away 2000. I have his cap, Lancashire Cricket Club tie and Manchester
City scarf hung up in the hall. I talk to him, I can feel him. I think about him a lot.
God bless him.

Woodsmoor to Manchester

I love going to Manchester,
and riding on this train.
Seeing all the people,
but they always look the same.

Everybody has got to go to work,
and do the best they can.
But as my Dad would say,
they've got faces like bad ham.

The market town of Stockport,
where every train has to stop.
With it's famous brick built viaduct,
the river Mersey starts it's drop.

I look through the window,
watch the sun rise over the peaks.
I never fail to say to myself,
God, this is a treat.

Here we are in Levenshulme,
once more green and grand.
Now you can go for a curry,
or listen to an Irish band.

The Eastlands Stadium,
built for the commonwealth games.
United have their theatre of dreams,
City, expectations.

We lived for a short time at 56 Energy St, Miles Platting which was close to the colliery.

I can see Bradford gas works,
I got coke there when I was a kid.
We had a coal fire back then,
mind you everyone did.

*Piccadilly station where the
Quality Street Gang turned back the Krays.
Go back to London and your jellied eels,
we won't stand your evil ways.

Over mighty London Road,
how it's changed in so few years.
No more Mazels electrical shop,
for valves to bring music to our ears.

There's the Palace Theatre,
we're coming into Oxford Road.
I sang there once with the Rolling Stones,
it was 1964.

So on to Deansgate Station,
once called Knott Mill'
I love coming into Manchester,
it always gives me a thrill.

*Piccadilly Station, the Kray's and the Quality Street Gang - there was also a large
Manchester CID squad Involved.

Shambles Square

This fine Tudor building,
The Old Wellington Inn, 1552,
Writer John Byron was born there,
In the year 1692.

Later came Sinclairs Oyster Bar,
About 200 years in fact,
Considering what they been through,
It's a wonder they're still in tact.

Moved twice from different locations,
A complicated engineering affair,
In the arms of the Mitre Inn and the Cathedral,
Settled nicely in Shambles Square.

Going Away Late

I'll be brown for Christmas,
You'll be as white as white as a sheet,
In the snow, I will glow,
You will just blend in.

I'll be brown for Christmas,
Factor two will make me look swell,
You'll still be white, but that's alright,
Next year, I'll take you as well.

The Lone Ranger

I don't want be the Lone Ranger,
Nobody knowing my name,
I don't want to be incognito,
But I want to be your claim to fame.

I don't want be the Lone Ranger,
Riding off into the sun,
On a big, fine white horse,
Silver bullets in my gun.

I don't want to be the Lone Ranger,
Nobody knowing who I am,
Always disappearing,
People saying who was that man.

Oceans Eleven

Running the show at Oceans Eleven,
About 1975,
Some nights it was pretty rough,
You just wanted to get out alive.

The carpet almost soggy,
In parts you would stick to the floor,
Some fights, mostly Friday,
Could involve fifty or more.

One night the Manager Jack Plant,
A fine and descent man,
I saw him guide the fight to the exit door,
To the Police, and a black Maria van.

Outside the battle raging,
I saw a brick come down on Jack's head,
Landed heavy and fractured his skull,
One of the reasons he's now dead.

But it was not always violent,
Most nights we had a good time,
Reg Coates, The Black Abbotts,
Great acts that spring to mind.

Thursday was men only,
With cabaret and exotic fun,
Strippers of all shapes and sizes,
Big Julie being the oddest one.

Once, stood next to one of the girls,
After her dancing and frolics,
I said what's the difference between looking and touching,
She said "A kick in the bollocks."

I learnt a lot at Oceans Eleven,
Although it led me astray,
I thought it was good at the time,
But I regret it to this day.

Oceans Eleven was on the junction of Dickenson road and Anson road. It used to be a
Birchpark Roller Skating Rink. I saw Gene Vincent there.

After Oceans Eleven it was Genevieve's, a disco. Then it became the rock venue
International One. I Remember seeing Rockin' Sydney from New Orleans there he wrote
Don't Mess With My ToTo. He sang it three times.

Now a very good Asian & Continental food shop. If only they knew.

Only Funerals Left

We used to see relatives at weddings,
Have a few drinks and a laugh,
Seems like nobody gets married any more,
Is it a thing of the past?

Now there's nothing left but funerals,
To meet the kin you've no time to visit,
Look around at your ageing family,
Think to yourself, it's not my turn yet is it?

So keep in touch with these people,
And don't leave it too late,
Because there will be one funeral you go to,
They'll be waiting for you at the gate.

Strike While The Iron Is Hot

You have got to make your life complete,
Don't let the grass grow under your feet,
If there is moonlight, and it feels right,
She probably feels the same way as you,
So don't miss this golden opportunity,
I know if it was me,
I'd grab the bull by the horns,
Accept full responsibility,
I know if it was me,
I'd strike while the iron is hot,
For he who hesitates is lost,
You've got to keep movin' don't look back,
Life's too short for that,
You've got to strike while the iron is hot.

Who knows when we'll dance again,
The band might go home,
What will we do then my love, is it the end my love,
I know I've had a drink, but I'll drive my car,
Go down town to a late night bar,
See how the money goes, we'll stay till they close,
Later on if we still feel good,
We'll go home and make love like never before,
Like never before,
Strike while the iron is hot,
For he who hesitates is lost,
You've got to keep movin' don't look back,
Life's too short for that,
You've got to strike while the iron is hot.

Confusion In Suburbia

Is that, what's his name over there, you know, he used to be married to that thin woman who did reki? Yes it is, I thought he was seeing that other woman...her with the two kids. I know who you mean, but that was ages ago. Didn't she run off with that big bloke, remember he had loads of money? They live in the south of France, at least I think they do. Hang on, that was her sister, she left him. He goes in the Crown, three children to look after. He's still on his own, or did I see him in the Indian having a curry with that younger woman. I couldn't tell if they were an item! May even have been his eldest daughter they grow up so quick nowadays.

Fancy a drink in the wine bar, we've not been in there for some time? Two glasses of red wine please. Don't turn round, but that couple in the corner, I didn't know they were together. He used to live with that red haired woman, they got divorced. He used to work abroad, she was seeing him while he was away. Didn't he come home early and catch them in bed, punched him, threw her out. I believe he lives with his first wife now. They don't come out much, not round here anyway. Bloody hell look who's just come in, I thought they had split up years ago, they look very well together. They did break up for a while, he went to live with that girl who worked in the shop around the corner. She went to live in London. Just shows you, they must be back together again.

I don't know, this place eh! Everybody's integrated, give it a few more years, everyone will be related.

Clan Members from 1963

Pete Bocking, Ex Fourtones, Pete Bocking 6
Johnny Hynes, Drums
Brian "Rainy" Day, Bass
Mitch Pickup, Bass
Darby O'Gill (Aussy), Guitar
Dave Smith, Ex-Measles, Guitar
John Kelman, Ex-Freddy Starr, 4 Just Men
Leo Larty, Drums.
Bernie Byrns, Drums
Stuart Syrett, Guitar
Alan" Fuzz"Unsworth (Clare), Guitar
Albi Sayers, Bass
Frank Renshaw, Guitar
Dave Buck, Drums
David Gleeve (Glez), Guitar
Alan Doyle, Guitar
John (Shed\Studios)
Derek "Lek" Lekenby, Guitar
Colin Lekenby, Guitar
Max Beasley, Drums
Mike Smith, Drums

Brendan Day, Drums
Kim Turner, Drums
Henry Quick, Drums
Paul Burgess, Drums
Dave Lunt, Bass
Nick Berry, Drums
Steve Williams, Bass
Phil Chapman, Sax
Mike Gilbourne, Drums
John Gibson, Bass
Dave Moss, Sax
Terry Morton, Guitar
Nicky Knott, Drums
Tony Kelly, Sax
Pete Hilton, Drums
Bob Cooke, Piano
Mo Crichlow, Bass
Eddie Edwards, Drums
Tony Bookbinder, Drums
Colin Larne,Drums

The line up at this time:
Graham Attwood, Saxophone
Dave Barrow, Bass
Steve Gibson, Drums
Gerry McLaughlin, Guitar

Thank Your Lucky Stars

Being on Thank Your Lucky Stars,
Back in 1963,
We thought "wow" this is it,
The world now at our feet.

Our record will sell now,
It'll be high in the charts,
But something was happening.
To upset the apple cart.

The Decca pressing plant on holiday,
No records to be had,
It was the way it worked then,
The only chance we had.

We met Mr Brian Mathew,
Janice gave it 5,
Bo Diddly and Freddy Cannon,
We all mimed, the show wasn't live.

John Leyton and Mike Berry,
The Duchess and Jerome,
The fabulous Tornados,
The Big Three wanted a lift home.

They said "Pete, our van as broken down,
we can't get back to the pool",
We took them all the way,
Help your pals was our rule

Not forgetting Johnny, Pete and Brian,
The Clan, they kept me going,
The mohair suits for that day,
They were made by Michael Cohen.

Jerome, Mike Berry, Pete Bocking,
Brian Day (Four Tornados), John
Lyton, The Duchess, Brian Matthew,
Johnny Hutchingson, Johnny
Gustafson, Brian Griffith, Big Three,
Bo Diddley and Freddy Cannon.
Johnny Hynes, me & Clem Cattini.

Coronation Street

I've just been sat in Roy's Rolls,
That's the café in Coronation Street,
While the actors chirped and learned their lines,
They gave me something to eat,
It's got to be authentic, it's got to look real,
They took some time getting it right,
So I finished off that really nice meal,
Sometimes in the Rovers Return,
Chatting and drinking strange beer,
People say what do you talk about,
Truth is we're miming, no-one can hear,
Often I walk along the famous street,
In sunshine and Manchester rain,
Some people would give their right arm,
Just to do the same,
Here I am with these lovely people,
I think to myself, blinkin' 'ek
I always have a very nice time
And then they send me a cheque!

There were some funny times in the Rovers. We were all set to film one day, on "action", Tony Little, who was stood at the bar, broke wind. Everybody fell about laughing. The director said settle down, and we'll do that again. Tony said "Do you want to leave the fart in?" He got away with it, he still does it today, he Street that is.

L to R: Me, Peter Armitage, Tony Little

The Big Three

The Beatles were the Beatles,
We all know they were fab,
But there was one Liverpool outfit,
Who didn't fall into the trap.

The voice of Johnny Gustafson,
Brian Griffiths, a wonder on guitar,
No nonsense drumming from Johnny Hutch,
They shone above all by far.

With home made amplification,
The whole gear didn't cost a lot,
But the sound they created,
Once seen, never forgot.

The Big Three didn't storm the charts,
Like some of their Liverpool mates,
But for me, and lots of others,
They were among the greats.

THE BIG THREE *Decca Records*

The Rocket

Riding along on this trolley,
I forgot my brolly,
I hope it doesn't rain today.

The news isn't all bad,
But then again I'm his dad,
Sometimes I struggle for something to say.

By the look in his eye
He's wondering why,
How it ever got to be this way.

He's got friends all around,
They get the lift from the ground,
I stand back and try to take it all in.

They all mean well,
But it's so hard to tell,
The best way for him to go.

So I ride on this Rocket,
I hope I can clock it,
The best solution for my faraway son.

But then I'm thinking, after all,
He is there for us all,
And St. Michael has done the best that he can.

The Rocket is a trolley bus (a bit like Blackpool, only funkier) that passes along Queen through Toronto. My son Nicholas in St. Michael's hospital (The Urban Angel) with a suspected broken back. He had been helping a friend paint his house and fell off the ladder onto the step. Ouch! July 2005.

Me and Nicholas in Toronto

Graceland

Big Llew and me went to Graceland,
It was the summer of '82,
To pay our respects to the King,
It was something we had to do.

Out of Washington on the east coast,
On the bus, Nashville bound,
Say hello to Hank and the boys,
In that good ole' country town.

Then back again on the Greyhound,
Now D.C. far behind,
Rode into Memphis Tennessee,
Graceland not hard to find.

We got to meet Uncle Vester,
The brother of Elvis's Father,
The King himself wasn't in,
He was in the garden.

After more than one Jack Daniels,
We headed for the Golden State,
Through Texas and Arizona
San Diego was our fate.

But we stopped in El Paso,
We drank Tequila in the middle of the night,
In a seedy bar full of Mexicans,
Got back to the bus a bit tight.

San Diego up to Frisco,
We crossed the mighty Golden Gate,
Then back to Los Angeles for the flight home,
We could not afford to be late.

American Airways to New York,
Then to Manchester across the pond,
We will come back to this wonderful country,
I hope it's not too long. (It wasn't)

Me, Uncle Vester and Elvis's cousin Jimmy.

Sad Café

People enthuse about Manchester bands,
From the past and the ones today,
But there is one group who aren't mentioned enough,
That's the fabulous SAD CAFÉ.

The powerful soulful voice of Paul Young,
In 2000 he sadly passed away,
My oh my, Every Day Hurts,
Without the fabulous SAD CAFÉ.

At Paul Young's funeral with my good friend Derek Brandwood (below), I was talking to Duggie James, telling him that my Dad had died. The next night we were playing at the Bull's Head, Duggie came and sang Ain't No Sunshine When HE'S Gone. I watched from the bar with tears in my eyes. It was very moving.

Derek Brandwood was mine and Paul Young's manager, he died in 2005. He was a good man, he always made me feel special and did his best for me, I really miss him.

At Derek's funeral, Duggie with his brother Barry on guitar, sang Dobie Grey's Drift Away, stood by the coffin, it was fabulous. The man should have been a star. Paul of course was a star, to me and lots of other people. He didn't get the credit he deserved in Mike and the Mechanics. It was Paul Carrak who got the attention, but it was "our" Paul who put energy and feel into their show.

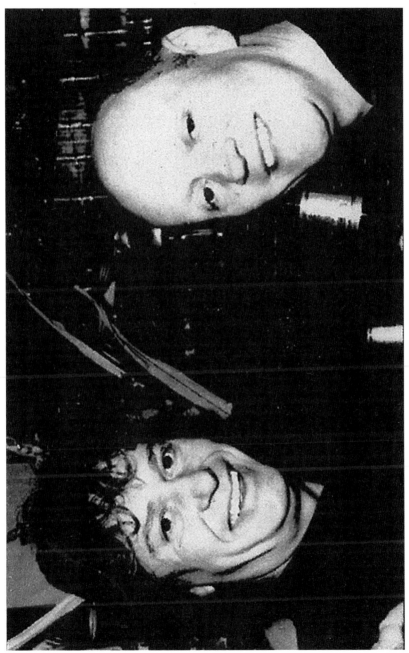

The late Paul Young, with Pete Maclaine celebrating the launch of KCLX Radio at Manchester's Sticky Fingers Restaurant, 1st Februay 1997.

Bunny's, Oldham Street 1957

Oldham street in the fifties,
Like An American Midwest town,
A bit like "Invasion of the body snatchers"
But with no "Pods" around.

Bunny's Like a U.S. Army and Navy store,
So glad it was there,
You could buy original Levi's jeans,
Blue ones like Elvis used to wear.

Once home with the famous denims,
Always one size too big,
Then sit in a bath of water,
They would shrink to a perfect fit.

Amazingly Oldham Street has stayed the same,
Even though Yates Blob Shop has gone,
The music getting closer,
The famous Castle Hotel battles on.

Half way down Oldham Street,
Stands Stevenson Square,*
On a corner was the Record Shop,
I bought my Elvis LP's there.

But now, a new Manchester band,
As to play at Night and Day,
Matt and Phreds if you're a jazzer,
Is the place to have your say.

There was Affleck and Brown,
A quite up market store,
Now the wondrous Afflecks Palace,
Something unique on every floor.

In the seventies on Oldham Street,
Stood the Guys and Dolls boutique,
In our fashion conscious city,
It was the place to meet.

Of course once on Oldham Street,
Stood a massive C&A,
I always thought it was a great store,
But still it faded away.

*Hilton Street runs through Stevenson Square. At the China Lane end, in the 1950s and early '60s there was a "works" that made donkey stones. In those day's people in terraced streets would "stone" their steps. Stones were given by rag and bone men in exchange for unwanted items of clothing. They would also give balloons to children. Rag and bone men would go around the streets on a horse and cart, sometimes just a push cart. The donkey stone place was owned by a Mr Gregory, I worked there the odd Saturday when I was a teenager, Mr Gregory, who's daughter Sheila is still a friend, had the first Jet petrol station in Manchester. It was on Great Ancoats Street.

I also remember other street traders. There was the "muffin man" on Saturday mornings. There was also a man who sold bundles of firewood.

Jutland Street

Like a secret Manchester joyride,
But it's there for all to see,
And, if you can find it,
I think you will all agree.

Heading down from Ducie Street,
Over thousands of shinny Victorian cobbles,
Race down about 40 degrees toward Store Street,
Bet any money, you get the colly wobbles.

My first trip down our steepest street,
It was about 1959,
In a blue and white Ford Zodiac,
Two girls and Eddie, he was a friend of mine.

That first time was the best,
But quite fast is what it takes,
Then it's like the end of the world,
Hoping the car as got good brakes.

So one Sunday afternoon get yourself down there,
With your girl, or give the kids a treat,
Just in case it's not there for ever,
Take the trip down Jutland Street.

Litter

I really hate litter,
Especially on the streets of the city,
People drop it unconsciously,
In fact it's quite a pity.

I went to Vancouver once,
No litter to be seen,
I don't think I've been anywhere,
That's kept so nice and clean.

So I thought I would offer my services,
Maybe a couple of days a week,
I could help keep my city tidy,
And get nice rosy cheeks.

I made myself an appointment,
And told them of my plan,
They said can you start on Monday,
You seem an enthusiastic kind of man.

I said is there a training scheme,
To show me right from wrong,
They said no there's no training scheme,
You'll pick it up as you go along.

The Day My Heart Stood Still

In hospital with pneumonia,
Tucked up in a bed,
They gave me two lots of tablets,
The right ones they said.

They said more tests had to be done,
That this is just the start,
But the medication wasn't right for me,
In fact it stopped my heart.

At the time I was sat up talking,
To a jolly passing nurse,
If not for this little angel,
It would have been a lot worse.

Had I been quietly reading,
Or lay down resting my head,
With no one noticing my monitor,
I quite easily could have been dead.

I remember feeling light headed,
Very peaceful and no pain,
A grey cloud coming over me,
I thought I'd never see the world again.

But my angel was quick thinking,
She pounded at my heart,
In no time the cardiac team were there,
They gave me brand new start.

So thank you Stepping Hill ,
I won't say or hear a bad word,
Because you are the reason,
I'm still walking on this earth.

Since that little mishap,
I see things in a different light,
Dare I say the grass is greener,
The sky even more bright.

The Sunday Times

The very first interview with a pop group,
By Robert Robinson, a very nice man,
To go into the Sunday Times,
Was in fact Pete Maclaine and the Clan.

Write Off

A friend of mine crashed his car,
But it was an old banger,
It wasn't a complete write off,
He turned the aerial back into a coat hanger.

Tommy Cooper

Ladies and Gentlemen, the one and only, Tommy Cooper

Still in the dressing room with a mic',
It could take up to five minutes,
People laughing not really knowing why,
It was one of his many gimmicks.

But when he walked on, and through the gate,
Laugh, we thought we'd never stop,
And then "bottle glass, glass bottle, bottle glass",
Didn't have to wait for the penny to drop.

Backstage though Mr Cooper,
Not as funny as you might think,
For many years he struggled through,
Fighting the demon drink.

We remember him with love and affection,
And of course the famous hat,
He had us all spellbound,
Just like that!

Bob Monkhouse

Mr Monkhouse, the most professional of comics,
The wittiest, most satirical,
Sometimes blue, but never rude,
The master of sophisticated material.

A man of many talents,
An accepted, wonderful ego,
Did you know he was also a cartoonist,
He drew Pansy Potter in the Beano.

**The Willows fabulous
Resident Show**

with

Pete Maclaine

The Willow Birds

The Christie Band

Tibb Street

In the 1950's and early '60s
Tibb Street was a magical place for me,
From Piccadilly through Smithfield Market,
There was always something to see.

There were little cafés and book shops,
Some with naughty magazines,
Scantily clad ladies showing parts of their bodies,
Of which I had never seen.

But the shop next door sold pets,
Little kittens and puppies on a sawdust floor,
All together in the window,
Today's society would certainly deplore.

You could buy a budgie or a canary,
A goldfish in a plastic bag,
An African grey, even a monkey,
I couldn't wait to go back.

Of course now part of the Northern Quarter,
The market and pets all gone,
But it still has it's own personality,
I'm sure will continue to go on.

Granddad Ted

He was actually called Edwin,
Same as my Dad and mine,
My Great Granddad also,
I was fourth in the line.

In his backyard in Ancoats,
He ran a betting shop,
Quite illegal at the time,
But the police found it hard to stop.

My Dad was his runner,
A lookout during the race,
Some who tried to cheat them,
Often got a punch in the face.

Back then times were hard,
Breaks didn't come too often,
But one finely did,
The family moved to a house in New Moston.

Granddad got a job at A.V. Roe,
He worked on the Vulcan bomber,
The forerunner of course for Concorde,
That supersonic plane no longer.

Granddad Ted and Grandma Ada were happy,
At 16 Chatwood Ave,
With six daughters and three sons,
The best time they ever had.

Cancer

It took M'Mam two years to die of cancer,
Still longing for a fag,
She was so full of morphine,
She turned a nasty shade of black.

Now

No energy left for revitalisation,
To continue with the fight,
It's okay in the daytime,
But just wait until the night.

Live now with passion,
Before you get too old,
Life is there for the taking,
You can't just put it on hold.

Tommy Allsup

When Buddy Holly went to see the Searchers,
John Wayne, walking his unique way,
He latched on to those now famous words,
Went home and wrote That'll Be The Day.

The Crickets, Curtis, Mauldlin and Allinson,
As we know Buddie's backing band,
After all those hit records,
They were not always close at hand.

On the fatal tour of 1959,
With Ritchie, Dion and the Bopper,
It was Waylon Jennings and Tommy Allsup,
Who helped Buddy become the show stopper.

It was Tommy who tossed the coin with Ritchie,
To decide who would fly on that plane,
The big Texan guitar player lost,
But lives on, and still plays to this day.

Waylon went into country music,
And later found Outlaw fame.
But the guy who played lead guitar on It's So Easy,
Hardly anyone remembers his name.

With my good pals Kevin Parrott and Mick Coleman,
We went to see Tommy in 2007,
He played guitar and told fascinating stories,
A great Rock 'n' Roll history lesson.

L to R: Me, Kev and Mick

Kevin & Mick are in fact, Brian & Michael. Hit recorders of Matchstalk Men, 1978. I wrote the follow up:

Salford Sunset
There's the Salford sunset,
Glowing all red,
But Lowry can't paint it,
The poor old bugger's dead.

It never got released.

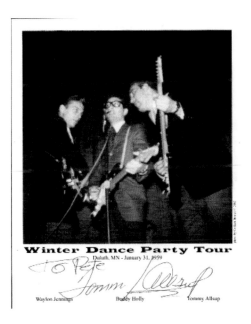

Tommy Allsup

The Midland Hotel

In 1970 we went to the Odeon,
To see David Crosby and Graham Nash,
Then across the road to the Midland Hotel,
In the rain a quick dash.

We went up to the 5th floor,
They had a very nice suite,
The boys in the band came in,
They were a pleasure to meet.

Crosby's sidekick was rolling joints,
The finest Californian weed,
They passed it all around,
We didn't have to plead.

But when it was our turn,
I think just for a laugh,
On the end of the joint,
He stuck on an acid tab.

By now this drug concoction,
Getting us both a bit stoned,
Graham said "Pete, where's Susan?",
I said she wanted to be alone.

We found her on the balcony,
Glassy eyed and very alone,
She said she wanted to jump off,
And fly herself home.

We're both pretty shaky now,
As they say, out of the game,
They apologised much later,
We didn't go down that road again.

The Prince of Wales AKA The Dead House

On the corner of Oldham Road and Grimshaw Lane,
What was just Manchester 10,
The closest pub to the canal,
But that was way back then.

People who had fallen into the cut,
Brought here to be revived,
Some were not so lucky,
Quite a few didn't survive.

A cosy little local pub,
A snug with smiling older ladies,
Men playing darts and crib,
They worked hard for their wages.

At the end the landlord Big Frank,
A rough and ready character,
The pub dirty and scruffy,
But that didn't seem to matter.

The favourite place for Wilson's dray men,
The brewery just across the road,
We would go there some afternoons,
To here funny stories they told.

A man came back with a cheese sandwich,
But he didn't linger,
"Frank I didn't want beetroot",
He said "It's not, I cut my bloody finger".

The toilets were rank and smelly,
In fact the whole place pretty bad,
But the beer Big Frank pulled,
One of the best pints I've ever had.

Albert Square

I love, when in the City,
To stand in Albert Square,
Gaze upon our Town Hall,
And people passing there.

This fabulous gothic building,
By Waterhouse, 1887,
The clock tower, 286 feet,
Proudly rising towards heaven.

Inside original murals,
By Ford Madox Brown,
Mosaic floors of busy bees,
Symbolising our industrial town.

A statue of good Prince Albert,
Keeping an ever watchful eye,
Over music festivals and Christmas markets,
Rain, and even clear blue sky.

J.Wippell & Co, specialist gents outfitters,
Looking south across the square,
This Victorian old-fashioned shop,
A great view, for the people working there.

So, I like to stand in Albert Square,
It can take me back in time,
To Whit walks, the Church Lads Brigade,
Marching under the Saint Marks sign.

Manchester and Home

Leaving Hania airport,
We kissed the sunshine goodbye,
On a Boeing 737,
To Manchester and home.

First over the sea of Crete,
Then the finger like Peloponnese,
With Italy on our port side,
To Manchester and home.

High above the Alps and onward,
Then the Rhine far below,
The forests like purple brocolii,
To Manchester and home.

Over France and gay Paris,
We can see the wonderful tower,
Then mighty London, our capital city,
To Manchester and home.

Coming down slowly over the peaks,
Kinder Scout, where I walk with my son,
Not far now over beautiful England,
To Manchester and home.

The Beetham Tower, Deansgate

Some people say the Beetham Tower,
Is not a pretty sight,
I think it looks great,
Especially shining in the night.

Housing the prestigious Hilton Hotel,
And the fabulous Bar 23,
Panoramic views over the city,
I'm as proud as I can be.

The mostly glass building itself,
Grey like Manchester rain,
But ready to change chameleon-like,
Whenever sunshine came.

The tower looks down on older buildings,
Ryland's, Royal Exchange, the Town Hall,
The Little Gem, St Anne's, the Cathedral send blessings,
Up to one that stands so tall.

So, this impressive imposing structure,
With olive trees on it's top floor,
Can Manchester keep up with progress,
Be successful, and maybe build some more.

YES!

The once tallest C.I.S. building,
Not quite left on the shelf,
Topped off in 1962,
I worked on it myself.

Another World

There are things going off, all over the place,
When will the news put a smile on my face,
How long can we take this abuse,
I try so hard, but it's no use.

This feeling can't just be inside me,
When will the majority set theirs free,
There is work to done, it's not too late,
Or have we sealed our very own fate.

It would take a whole lot of money, to inhabit the moon,
We had better hurry, it can't be too soon,
If you've got too much don't be shy to give,
My great, great, grandkids, will need somewhere to live.

I'm Alive

My baby loved Elvis,
Ricky Nelson too,
She's only three steps from heaven,
When Eddie comes into view.

Bobby Darin when he was rockin'
She thought he was great,
Playing Gene Vincent records,
She stayed up very late.

Johnny Burnett had her dreamin'
She wants to be Buddy's Peggy Sue,
I'll have to do something special,
To make her dream of me too.

I'm not too bothered about these rockers,
Even though she loves them with pride,
The fact is they're all dead,
But me, I'm still alive.

Arrivederci

I'm leaving Rome,
On my way home,
I said arrivederci, for the last time.

I've done my best,
Now I know I've been blessed,
To see this city, always an ambition of mine.

The Ragu and Pasta,
I couldn't eat any faster,
Washed down with Italian wine.

This city of churches,
Every one was worth it,
Of course St Peter's, just sublime.

Now that I'm home,
They say all roads lead to Rome,
So maybe, arrivederci, one more time.

Hania Crete

In a Venetian harbour,
We walked hand in hand,
Looking for a restaurant,
One cheap, but grand.

I looked across the table,
You stuffed risotto in your face,
Then I saw you smiling,
I had fish, chips and peas on my plate.

The Bodega

The Bodega on Cross Street,
With it's beautiful mahogany bar,
Jazz greats would play there,
Drawing fans from near and far.

Humphrey Lyttleton, Chris Barber,
Acker Bilk and many more,
In the fifties, these jazz giants,
Had them queuing at the door.

But later in that decade,
When this music began to fade,
Rock 'n' Roll was taking over,
Nothing could stand in it's way.

Friday nights Paul Beattie and the Beats,
A small fee to get in,
Once inside people jumpin' and jivin',
It was always full to the brim.

Trad jazz was still featured,
Mostly on Sundays with big names,
Tuesday country and Western,
The Hillbilly Bandits, hoping for fame.

The corner of Cross St. and Back Pool Fold, where the Bodega was. At the top is where
the Red Barn restaurant & Pygmalia were.

Other nights there were local groups,
The Four tones with Bocking, Clarke and Nash,
The Coasters, Jerry Lee and the Staggerlees,
Nobody cared if the songs clashed

The Dreamers with the effervescent Freddie,
Johnny Peters and the Jets,
Everybody having fun and laughing,
Manchester nights I'll never forget.

But as the sixties rolled by,
The fabulous bar was taken down,
The Bodega turned into a disco,
It was called The Top of the Town.

But this old Manchester venue,
Was never quite the same,
With the "Red Barn" next door,
The DJ was Gary Laine.

40 Shades of Blue

There are 40 shades of blue in our bathroom,
Johnny Cash had 40 shades of green,
There are 40 shades of blue in our bathroom,
41, when I go for a wee.

Manchester United, 1983

A friend of mine Frank Renshaw, an avid supporter, wrote Glory Glory Man United. The recording was at Yellow 2 in Stockport. Frank was the singer with The Hermits, they were working away at the time. He very kindly asked me to do the vocals and see the team through the session, which of course, I did. Frank's son Lee, and friend Phil Keene also sang on the record. Although I didn't get a credit, I did get paid, and that was okay by me. It was great fun, and the closest I have been to the Hit Parade. The team did sign the word sheet for me, I'll let you sort the names out yourselves. The picture disc will help. I am still proud to have been involved in this little piece of history.

Frank wrote lots of great songs and was a founder member of Stockport band "The Toggery Five". They were managed by Michael Cohen, owner of The Toggery, a clothing shop in Mersey Square. They sold the original "Anillo and Davide" Cuban heeled Beatle boots, all the groups bought them the fab four included. They cost £4.19. 6. Michael made leather jackets for the Beatles in 1961. Still a good friend, he also managed The Hollies. Not from Stockport, or even Manchester but Salford and Colne. Graham Nash and myself worked at The Toggery together for a short time.

The Toggery Five did include the one and only Paul Young, later with cult Manchester band Sad Café. Then onto Mike and the Mechanics, unfortunately Paul, one of our great singers and showmen, died in 2000. He will always be missed.

GLORY GLORY MAN UNITED
GLORY GLORY MAN UNITED
GLORY GLORY MAN UNITED
AND THE REDS GO MARCHING ON ON ON

JUST LIKE THE BUSBY BABES IN DAYS GONE BY,
WE'LL KEEP THE RED FLAGS FLYIN' HIGH,
YOU'RE GONNA SEE US SCORE FROM FAR AND WIDE,
YOU'RE GONNA HEAR THEM AS THEY SING WITH PRIDE.

UNITED, MAN UNITED
WE'RE THE BOYS IN RED AND WE'RE ON OUR WAY TO WEMBLEY.
WEMBLEY, WEMBLEY WE'RE THE FAMOUS MAN UNITED
AND WE'RE GOING TO WEMBLEY.

WEMBLEY, WEMBLEY WE'RE THE FAMOUS MAN UNITED
AND WE'RE GOING TO WEMBLEY.

IN 77 IT WAS DOCHERTY
ATKINSON WILL MAKE IT 83.
AND EVERYONE WILL KNOW JUST WHO WE ARE
THEY'LL BE SINGING QUE SERA SERA.

UNITED, MAN UNITED
WE'RE THE BOYS IN RED AND WE'RE ON OUR WAY TO WEMBLEY.
WEMBLEY, WEMBLEY WE'RE THE FAMOUS MAN UNITED
AND WE'RE GOING TO WEMBLEY.

WEMBLEY, WEMBLEY WE'RE THE FAMOUS MAN UNITED
AND WE'RE GOING TO WEMBLEY.

GLORY, GLORY MAN UNITED
GLORY, GLORY MAN UNITED
GLORY, GLORY MAN UNITED
AS THE REDS GO MARCHING ON
GLORY, GLORY MAN UNITED
GLORY, GLORY MAN UNITED
GLORY, GLORY MAN UNITED
AS THE REDS GO MARCHING ON ON ON
GLORY GLORY ETC... cont...

Manchester United, 1983 Cont.

The Toggery Five had Alan Doyle on guitar who later, along with Dave Barrow (in the Clan now) backed Alvin Stardust. Alan is now in The Emperors of Rhythm with old rocker Charlie Barker, a great band.

In the 70's Frank, me and our then wives, Pauline and Sue formed "Boggy Remedy". Not for too long, but I had to get the caricature in (overleaf). It was good fun.

Glory Glory Man United still plays the team on at Old Trafford. Nice one.

The Silence, 2008

It was a bright and sunny afternoon,
Old Trafford was full to the brim,
Three thousand Manchester City fans,
That's all they could let in.

It was fifty years since Munich,
Quite a sombre affair,
A very moving experience,
In the crowd, in the pub, armchair.

The media expecting some kind of disturbance
That there would be no respect shown,
But I had a feeling in my heart
That Manchester would look after it's own.

When it came to the minutes silence,
Not a sound could be heard,
For the whole sixty seconds
It was the quietist place on earth.

I remember nineteen fifty-eight,
And the pictures in the Evening News,
People staring with tears in their eyes,
They couldn't believe it was true.

Today, City were buzzing and up for it,
United didn't get into their play,
It was 2-1 for the blues,
But it was the silence that won the day.

Boogie Remedy

Boogie Remedy

Are four happy people who have an irresistible urge to make others feel the same, through their music and personalities, good singing and lots of laughs.

Frank Renshaw and Pete Maclaine have known each other since the early group days, and enjoyed success in all aspects of the business.

Frank was originally with the Toggery Five and later as Young and Renshaw became an established songwriter, Blue Mink are amongst artists who have recorded Frank's songs. In February Frank and his wife Pauline came back to England after six months spent working in America.

Pete Maclaine and the Clan were well known up and down this country and abroad on TV and Radio. Pete then stayed in Manchester for a while compering at local night spots and working in recording studios. Sue, Pete's wife and Pauline have also worked as backing vocalists on various artists records, including Wayne Fantana.

The two fellas and their wives got on so well together sharing the same sense of humour —MAD— and the same taste in modern music, they unanimously decided to form:

Harry Goodwin

1964, Top Of The Pops started,
In an old church on Dickenson Road,
Like a magnet for pop stars,
Many stories have been told.

They came from all over the world,
Like moths to a flame,
To sing in front of dancing Mancunians
All searching for TV fame.

Fabulous pictures were taken,
For Manchester posterity,
All by the one and only Harry Goodwin,
The uncrowned king of pop photography.

Harry Goodwin

The famous Harry Goodwin portrait of George Best

All in vain

You took my money,
You took my house,
You took my cat,
To catch your mouse.

You took a picture,
That was hanging on the wall,
I'll have to redecorate,
And that's not all.

You took my watch,
On its Albert gold chain,
Now it's gone,
It was all in vain.

Check the time,
When you're all alone,
I visualise your face,
All I see is stone.

New Mills, Bees Knees

When we played in New Mills,
We hardly ever got a clap,
They called us Townies,
In fact some said we were crap.

Maybe it's because I joked,
That there wasn't much difference,
Between that little town,
And the Burt Renolds film Deliverance.

We came off stage to no response,
A man, who dressing as a tramp he had mastered,
Stopped Atty, pointing to his sax he said,
"bet you can't play Apache on that bastard".

Que Sera Sera

When I was just a little boy,
I asked my mother what would I be,
Will I be handsome, will I be rich,
Here's what she said to me,
"Don't be stupid".

Nash at 67

There's a famous seaside resort called Blackpool,
Noted for fresh air, and fun,
Where Mr and Mrs Nash had Graham,
A lovely little son.

When they moved to Salford,
They took him to Belle Vue Zoo,
But he didn't get eaten by a lion,
He just grew and grew and grew.

With great success in the music world,
He must have thought he was in heaven,
But he worked hard and got it right,
I tell you, he looks bloody good at 67.

Going to Bed

You climb into you bed,
Hoping for a good night's sleep,

The one you love,
Just within reach,

Some nights filled with passion,
But most, sweet slumber,

Lets face it my friend,
We're not getting any younger.

Roger Tweedale

Mr Roger Tweedale,
A more smiling face you'll never see,
He always took it with him,
Even watching Rochdale F.C.

But! Hey Mister Postman,
What does your bag hold,
Letters for empty houses,
Containing fictitious souls.

Only your friends,
The ones close at hand
Knew you were a drummer,
In a great rockin' band.

Not only a drummer,
But funny as well,
In your GPO uniform,
Nobody could tell.

God bless Roger Tweedale,
A nicer person hard to find,
When in the Rock 'n' Roll heaven,
Say hello to some friends of mine.

Roger was the drummer with the Royal Variety Show Band and rock band Oscar. He played on numerous recordings, including the number one hit, Matchstick Men. For 16 years, Roger was the Postman on Coronation Street. God bless him.

Leaving School

It was 1957,
The year I left school,
I was glad it was all over,
Now I could make my own rules.

No more to be told,
Not to wear my drainpipes,
Plenty of summertime left,
I could live my own life.

Maybe we all thought that,
We were only fifteen,
It was all rock 'n'roll,
A classic teenage dream.

I knew very soon,
I would have to get a job,
Earn some money, pay my way,
Not become a slob.

M'Mam got me an interview,
With CWS Engineers,
An apprenticeship for heating and welding,
It would last for five years.

For the first six months,
They sent me to Trafford Park,
It was a long way from Chadderton,
I left, and arrived home in the dark.

My teacher was an old Millwright,
His name was Jack Wignall,
It was the time of the mighty ship canal,
I was there to witness it all.

Constructed in 1894,
To bypass Liverpool docks rising prices,
Ocean going ships sailed into the city,
Bringing Manchester richer prizes.

So there I was in the big wide world,
My school days not too far behind,
But the men who taught me right from wrong,
A better education in life hard to find.

My work boots, my first vision of photography when I was about sixteen. Helping my Dad
in the garden.

Manchester Beer

I love going to the pub,
And me being a bitter drinker,
You can keep that lager stuff,
Especially in the dead of winter.

It's not just drinking the beer,
It's the anticipation of how it's going taste,
And after the first mouth full,
Will it put a smile on my face.

Threlfalls, Grove & Whitnall's,
Now of course, long gone,
They say Chester's was a fighting beer,
It's reputation carries on.

Wilson's brewery, Newton Heath,
I remember it's hoppy smell,
A distinctive Manchester beer,
I drank pints of it as well.

Boddingtons, always an enjoyable drink,
When brewed at it's home in Strangeways,
Has it changed, or is it psychological,
Or just stuck in our ways.

Joseph Holt, famous Manchester beer,
Once the cheapest pint in the in country,
They say it's an acquired taste,
So I drank it, I drank, I drank it.

Then there's Hyde's Anvil,
A really bright session pint,
Nowhere better than the Nursery Inn,
We've had many a fabulous night.

Strangest pub name: "Help The Poor Struggler", the landlord being one Albert
Pierrepoint, the hangman.

Manchester Beer II

That very old pub the Lass 'o' Gowrie on Charles Street,
Brews very fine distinctive numbered ale,
Visit the Marble Arch on Rochdale Road,
Their own beer will always impress without fail.

Sometimes going into a strange pub,
Half the bar staff don't know what they're doin',
And you have to say "don't pull it like that,
that's another pint you're going to ruin".

I know they think I'm a moaning old sod,
I try not to get up tight,
But if I'm paying two to three quid for a pint,
I want it delivered, just right.

I loved Sunday lunchtime with M'Dad,
12 till 2 in in the pub,
A good chat, a couple of pints,
Then home for roast beef and Yorkshire pud.

Victor Brox

The one and only Victor Brox,
His translucent skin,
Twinkling blue eyes,
His warmth from within.

With his long grey beard,
The battered old trumpet,
His home made guitar,
Anyone else would have slung it.

This unique entertainer,
Who I can call my friend,
This wandering blues musician,
Victor Brox, Manchester legend.

Clan Days Over, For Now

A couple of months into '64,
Me and the Clan coming to the end,
It was a difficult time,
Especially involving friends.

We were getting pretty shaky,
With not too good reports,
Bocking and Rainy had gone,
Johnny Hynes holding the fort.

Maybe we should have gone in a different direction,
Using the musical ability within,
To this fine trio of musicians,
Pop music was getting a little thin.

But management had other ideas,
Me, using a different band,
That being "The Four Just Men",
And they were close at hand.

After a while, we made EMI studios,
To Ron Richard's, the Hollies' producer,
But they wanted to use a collective name,
I said "In that case, carry on without me sir",

They did and were quite successful.
Jam side down again. HA!

PETE MACLAINE AND THE FOUR JUST MEN
Kennedy Street Enterprises Ltd.
Kennedy House
14 Piccadilly, Manchester 1
CENtral 5423

DECCA RECORDS

Left for Dead

It was a dark and rainy Saturday night,
The end of '69,
We'd closed the show at a social club,
Going down just fine,

Into our Vauxhall Ventura,
John, Dave* and my wife Sue,
Off to a late night cabaret show,
Back then the thing to do,

We went to the Riverboat, Lower Broughton,
We'd worked there before,
Wolf Montgomery was the compere,
We knew the people on the door.

Sue and her friend Carol were dancing,
Two guys tried to split them up,
When they refused, I had to intervene,
To say the least, things got a little rough.

I caught the first blow on my chest,
My return smashed into his face,
Then it was like a scene from a cowboy film,
Fighting all over the place.

I ended up not too worse for wear,
As the bouncers took control,
The gang which it now was,
Were finely slung out onto the road.

We settled down for a few more drinks,
Adrenalin still running through our veins,
When it was time to say goodnight,
We had forgotten the violent exchange.

*John Kellman was a guitarist ex-Freddy Starr & and the Midnighter's and Four just Men.
Dave Smith, guitarist and vocalist ex-Measles.

We made our way down the stairs,
To the dimly lit exit,
What was waiting outside,
We certainly didn't expect it.

They stood in a semi circle,
In the shadows, out of the light,
I couldn't make out their faces,
Just clenched fist, ready to fight.

Dave and John were knocked to the ground,
Both held away from the fray,
For some reason I was the target,
I was their only prey.

Sue looking on in disbelief,
Thinking, why did we come to this place,
No punches to my body,
Each one rained on my face.

It was all over in no time,
I was left in a pool of blood,
Somebody had called for an ambulance,
I'm sure they came as fast as they could.

When they arrived on the scene,
Sue almost fainted when she heard what they said,
They told her to expect the worst,
"We think he might be dead".

I was taken to Salford Royal hospital,
Woke up in a quite a comfy bed,
With some very nice people,
Looking after my very swollen head.

Left for Dead Cont.

Apart from cuts and bruises,
Fractured cheek bones, broken nose,
Lacerations in my mouth created ulcers,
You don't even want one of those.

Relatives and friends who came to see me,
Walked past my unrecognisable face,
I was there four nights and days,
I couldn't have been in a better place.

Thanks.

THE CLAN

Things that stuck in my head

On my way to Granada TV one morning at about 7.30, I noticed a tramp stuffing his belongings into a black bag after his night on a bench. I felt sorry for him, so I went over and asked him if he would like the sandwich I had made for my lunch. He looked up at me with his ice-blue eyes, through bushy grey eyebrows and matching beard and said "What's on it?", I said "It's pastrami with sliced beef tomatoes and fresh rocket on Marks and Spencer granary bread". He said "No, you're alright mate".

For me to learn a new "old" song now, it would have to be "Tequila".

On the early morning train to the city, it stopped just before Piccadilly Station. The guard came out and said, "Sorry there's been a hold up". I stood up and said "It's probably Butch and Kid again". I got nothing, it was 7.15am.

At a gig one night in 2009, an attractive woman, about my age, came up to me and said "I used to see you at the Oasis Club in 1962, I was the one who dropped my chips when I had an orgasm".

Some friends of mine wanted me to decorate their bedroom, so I went to see it. There was a mirror on the ceiling, my friend said to me "take no notice of that, it doesn't work any more". I said to his wife, "would you like me to paint the back of a younger man on it?".

A friend of ours at the bar in the Nursery ordered a pint of Guinness, his girlfriend said to him "If you have another pint, there is no sex for you tonight". He turns to the barmaid and says "Make it a half, and sack the foreplay".

Little Richard

1956, there it was, The Girl Can't Help It. We saw Eddie Cochran singing Twenty Flight Rock, Gene Vincent and the Blue Caps perform the incredible Be Bop A Lula and of course the mighty Little Richard with The Girl Can't Help It and She's Got It with his fantastic band. Can you imagine six years later, I'm in a dressing room in New Brighton, with Mr Vincent, Mr Richard and The Beatles (Although I had met Gene before at the Oasis). Gene was there to introduce Little Richard. I remember he wore a dark blue mohair suit. I told him that I did an impression of him in my act. I asked did he mind, he looked at me with those eyes and said "As long as you don't take the mickey out of ole' Gene", I still do it.

All the top scouse bands went on (I was the only Mancunian on the show, that's including the Dakota's), then the Beatles, it was of course an Epstein promotion.

Time for Little Richard. We were all excited, everyone who had been on, all waiting to see live, the one and only Little Richard.

Expecting the band on the records and in the film to be with him, we got a surprise - no brass section, just a fabulous drummer and bass player, a Hammond organist who just happened to be a sixteen year old Billy Preston, with the longest fingers I had ever seen. Mr Richard on piano and leaping around the stage like a wild man. They were fantastic.

After all that we had to go on "follow that?...impossible". We were halfway through our first number when my microphone went off, I couldn't believe it when Little Richard came out and handed me his microphone.

MERSEYSIDE'S GREATEST-EVER ROCK SPECTACULAR
HEADED BY AMERICA'S FABULOUS
LITTLE RICHARD

★ ★ ★ WITH ★ ★ ★

THE BEATLES
—AT THE—
TOWER BALLROOM
NEW BRIGHTON
OCT. 12 - 1962

★ ★ ★ ALSO APPEARING ★ ★ ★

THE BIG THREE - PETE MACLAINE - BILLY KRAMER
LEE CURTIS - RORY STORM - THE MERSEY BEATS
THE UNDERTAKERS - GUS TRAVIS - THE FOUR JAYS

(161)

Little Richard Cont.

By this time people were slowly leaving, it had been a long night. Later back stage I thanked "Little", we were mates now for what he did. He asked me to go back to America with him. I knew nothing about him being gay, not in those days. Still, nice to be asked.

Touring with the Stones

Touring with the Stones,
It was 1963,
It was fun, exciting,
Jumpin' jiving,
Adrenalin pumpin'
The joints were rockin,
I couldn't imagine it stopping,
Let it go on forever,
And the good times last,
Girls were screaming,
For me and the lads.

Bill Wyman and Brian Jones, who I got quite friendly with, took me to their office for me to consider recording some songs written by Jagger and Richards. I didn't choose any (I know, I was young and stupid - good time though), but Andrew "Loog" Oldham asked me to do a recording of the Hank Snow classic country song Nobody's Child. We went to Regent Sound where the Stones did all their early R&B tracks. On piano was John Paul Jones (later of course with Led Zepplin) with Keith Shepherd on guitar. I still have it on tape - I sound about twelve. A sad song.

They were all great, then we went for a pint and that was it. I shared the bill with The Rolling Stones at the Palace Theatre, My band then was the Four Just Men. They always loved my impression of Gene Vincent. I Still do it.

Come Outside

May 1962 and Come Outside by Mike Sarne and Wendy Richards was sitting at the top of the Hit Parade. A strange combination really, Mr Sarne a Russian language graduate and Miss Richards an up and coming young actress. During the summer of that year they did a mini tour of the north west. The Dakotas, with their experience backing top acts, got the gig. I did the first half of the show, then introduced the top of the bill. We were playing Southport and before the show we all went to have some fun on the fair. Some of us were on the roller coaster, quite a good one. We were racing to the end of the ride when Mike Sarne, who was sat in front me, suddenly pushed the safety bar forward and stood up waving to Wendy and the lads down below. We were getting very close to the tunnel with a warning notice, "REMAIN SEATED". I reached up and grabbed his collar and pulled him back down into his seat just before we disappeared into the black hole of the tunnel.

When the car finely came to a halt, Mike was the same colour as an old "New Musical Express". I was feeling good that I had almost certainly saved his life, and about the money I had saved on dry cleaning. He was very grateful. I met him a couple of times later, the first thing he said was "remember Southport?". I do, but not just for that incident. I had much nicer memories of that little tour. Wendy Richards was a very nice young lady, we got on very well together. She of course, went on to a very successful career. Wendy did invite me down to her mothers pub in London. I don't think it was in the "East End" though. I never made it. God Bless her.

JUDGES' CHOICE. The panel of four judges headed by Mike Sarne and Wendy Richard, and helped by Pete Maclaine and Tony Mansfield of the Dakotas, picked the winners of the third heat of the Southport English Rose contest yesterday afternoon. Les girls, left to right, are Wendy Richard, Delyse Humphreys (reserve), Valerie Martin and Susan Pritchard (joint winners) and Cheryl Driscoll (reserve). Mike Sarne is centre back.

The Cresta Ballroom

The Cresta Ballroom was in fact Newton Heath Palais. It was just off Oldham Road behind the Ceylon Cinema that was on Thorpe Road. When M'Mam took me to the pictures, which was quite often, it was here or the Playhouse on Oldham Road. Sometimes if I went on my own and the film was an 'A' meaning you had to be with an adult, I would stand outside and ask someone, "could you take me in please?". I can't imagine doing that happening today. The Palais had dances on Saturday night, with at least a ten piece band. In the late fifties and into the sixties on Sunday afternoons they had a DJ and groups on. It was great, teenagers could have Sunday dinner, then leave their Mam and Dad asleep on the settee and go for a bop, all teetotal. The place was run by Mr and Mrs Hunt and their son Alan. The first time I saw Dave Berry and the Cruisers and Jimmy Crawford and the Ravens (both from Sheffield) was at the Cresta Ballroom, I loved it, all the local groups, DJ's (sometimes Ian Hamilton) and lots of girls!

The suit I am wearing in the photo opposite, I bought from The Boston Man Shop, St. Anne's square, now long gone. I treated myself for my 18th birthday. When our drummer Ebber left, we had changed our name from the Drovers to the The Four Teens.

It was in Barratts music shop on Oxford Street, where all the young groups used to meet. We heard of a young drummer Tony Mansfield, Bookbinder really. We went to see him one night, he was the drummer in the dance band at The Cresta Ballroom. We asked him to join us and he did. Not much long after that, name change again, this time to the Dakotas. I was still Pete Wetton. Happy days.

As the Four Teens we recorded Teenager In Love and Don't Tell Me Your Troubles. Recorded straight onto 10 inch disc at Johnny Roadhouse's above the shop. We were one of the first groups to play Bernard Manning's Embassy club. I did it many times later in cabaret and got to know Bernard quite well over the years, good man.

Used Car Salesmen

Well I looked at my car just the other day,
I thought to myself what a sight,
I'm gonna go to the bank and borrow some money,
And buy one that looks real nice.

So I cleaned my old car the best I could,
It looked quite shinny and new,
I picked one fine Sunday morning,
And took it to a garage or two.

I drove around then I parked my car,
At the back of a second hand lot,
When I got out, before I'd closed the door,
The salesman was there like a shot.

With his sheepskin coat, and his hat to match,
His face was red and round,
With an unlit cigar stuck between his teeth,
He was weighing my car up and down.

He said good morning can I help you,
What kind of car are you looking for,
Here's a nice one, one lady owner,
She didn't drive it too far.

Only to church on Sunday morning,
Her prayer book was on the back seat,
Then he tossed me the keys, said take it for a spin,
You'll find it drives a treat.

If you don't like that, what about this,
I can see what kind of man you are,
To tell you the truth I've been driving it myself,
It's a real enthusiast car.

Its got five forward gears, radial tyres'
It takes the bends so well'
I'd like to reduce the price sir'
But yours wont be easy to sell.

If not that, what about this, the bargain of the week'
I'll take yours off your hands, give you six months tax'
And a brand new MOT.

Used car salesmen they're a breed alone,
Three or four, or more in a bar, they have a language all of their own,
They talk monkeys, oncers and ponies, letters from A to A,
And when the boys get together,
You cant understand a single word they say.

Now I'm not the man, to nail on your hat,
I suppose you think that's funny,
Just step into the office sign on the dotted line,
and please, give me some money.

Stockport Market

Picture below as a four piece - Lto R: Albi Sayers, me, Stuart Syrett, Brendan Day plus "Atty" who was away in Saudi Arabia.

The picture opposite as a five piece - L to R: Bernie Byrnes, me, Albi Sayers, "Atty" and Alan Unsworth.

The line up change again, one year at Monroe's wine bar - Gerry Mclaughlin, Dave Barrow and Brendan Day. This line up plus "Atty" moved to The Bull's Head. Brendan had to leave and Max Beasley took over on drums. We were at The Bull's Head, through sickness and health, rain, snow, cold and hot for 16 years.

The Bull's Head

I was stood one night contemplating putting the gear away after a gig. People were leaving, laughing and waving good night. Dave Barrow says "look at them, they've had value for peanuts".

Graham Attwood, looking at my wrist says "what's that Pete" I tell him it's a friendship bracelet. He said "did you find it?".

Dave again, getting near to the end of the first spot he calls me and says "how long to go?" then lifting his almost empty glass up says "I've only got a song an' half left".

I had just got back from Toronto (I had been to see my son Nicolas) and I was telling the people at the Bull's Head about being up the CNN tower. I said when I was at the top I got the "willies". Then I said, if men get the "willies" what do women get. Dave the bass player says "the house".

At the Bulls Head one very full night, I had to ask some girls to move their table back about six inches. One of them said "Is that a male six inches, or a female six inches?"

This is another "Barrowism". One night, putting the gear away the band were talking amongst ourselves. To attract our attention, somebody knocked on a large flight case. Dave, as quick as a flash said, "Two minutes, Mr Clitheroe". It's great being old, Jimmy Clitheroe was a very small entertainer. He had his own radio show in the '50s.

The Bull's Head II

One night I jokingly said to Dave Barrow "we've got a gig at the 99 Club, Barrow-in-Furness". He said "I'm not going to the 99 Club, even for a thousand pounds and a free curry, I hate that place". I said to him, "do you realise, when you die and you are cremated, you will actually be Barrow In Furness!". He said "You'd better bury me then".

Do you know for guitar players, Eddie Cochran was born in Albert Lea, Minnesota. Spooky. Albert Lea was born December 21st 1943 in Leominster, Herefordshire.

It was Bob Troup who wrote Route 66 and not Chuck Berry as many people seem to think. He also wrote The Girl Can't Help It for Little Richard. There was also a Mrs Troup, who was in fact Julie London. While we're at it, the guitarist on Cry Me A River was Barney Kessel.

"See you Wednesday" picture opposite, Max left the band and Steve Gibson came in.

Opposite below, first night at the boar's head, 1982. With Bill "Butty", Stuart Syrett, Graham Attwood, Dave Barrow, Eddie Edwards and Frank Renshaw. The line up changed up to 1989.

Dave Barrow, butter wouldn't melt....

PETE MACLAINE
AND THE CLAN

binson's   BULLS HE

SEE YOU WEDNESDAY

My Friend, Stan Gibson

The Kippax coming down. Old Trafford in those days, had lots of trouble with their pitch. The story goes, and I believe it to be true, that the many award winning Stan - trying to help his fellow groundsmen - gave them lots of Maine Road worms.

I became friends with Stan and his family when I was the compere at The City Social Club.

First Port of Call

When going into Manchester,
Looking for a first port of call,
There's one little place to aim for,
I suggest it above all.

Almost on the junction,
Of Portland and Princess Street,
Like a terraced house turned into a pub,
I can assure you of the treat.

Once up the steps and inside,
Squeeze your way to the bar,
Just two hand pumps to serve you,
The smallest in the world by far.

Always full of smiling faces,
From the landlord and all his staff,
The atmosphere will get you,
I guarantee you'll have a laugh.

Settle down with your drinks,
In one of the snug like rooms,
Wintertime there's blazing fires,
You'll never want to move.

Surrounded by photographs,
Some very old and some new,
Pictures of football teams,
Both red and the blue.

There's one of the Busby Babes,
Sir Matt and swinging George Best,
Mercer, Lee, Bell and Summerbee,
Manchester teams on the crest.

You know now I love this place,
Have told you, no I haven't,
I might see you there sometime,
In the famous Circus Tavern.

Johnny Kidd & The Pirates

If you're writing about things in your life and you've worked with the fabulous Johnny Kidd and the Pirates, it's got to be mentioned. I first met them in 1961 at the Oasis Club. The pirates line up then was Johnny Spence - Fender bass, Frank Farley - drums and the mighty inspirational Mick Green - guitar.

Pete Maclaine and the Dakotas, dare I say, were nice, slick and polished with fancy routines. Johnny and the Pirates were rough, edgy, exciting and different to the other groups up north. I loved them, still do. Their van was an old ambulance, not just for their gear (which was not too bulky then) but also had mattresses in and if they didn't have anywhere to stay they slept in it, sometimes not alone!

Johnny (real name Fred Heath) died in a car crash on the road between Bury and Radcliffe, Lancashire in 1966. A great loss. He left a string of great recordings, the greatest being Shakin' all over, his own song. The dynamic guitar solo was session player Joe Moretti, with Clem Cattini I believe on drums.

Unfortunately Mick Green, who had also played guitar with amongst others The Dakotas, Englebert Humperdinck and Paul McCartney, died early in 2010. God bless him.

The Cavern, Liverpool 2005

One night in Liverpool,
A great night at the Cavern,
Stars still shining,
I never thought it could happen.

How could they get it together,
But I'm glad someone did,
The original Crickets and Haley's Comet's,
And all for fifteen quid.

Franny Beecher

Graham Attwood

The Crickets

King of the Travelling Fairground, '58

One warm summer Saturday night,
I'll take you to the fair,
I'm good with an air rifle,
I'll win you a Teddy Bear.

We'll go on the Waltzer,
And spin round and round,
Watch out for the greasy guy,
King of the travelling fairground.

The music still inside my head,
At 78 R.P.M.
Big thick records crashing down,
I loved every one of them.

Here he comes now,
He'll give us an extra spin,
With sideburns just like Elvis,
Do I really want to be like him?

He's stood there not holding on,
Teenage hearts will pound,
But he wont be here next week,
King of the travelling fairground.

My Fairground Top Ten:
Whole Lotta Shakin' Goin' On
Good Golly Miss Molly
All Shook Up
That'll Be The Day
Rip It Up
Great Balls Of Fire
Sweet Little Sixteen Oh Boy
Ain't That a Shame
Hound Dog

The Fourmost

Of all the groups in Liverpool I was most friendly with the 4Jay's. They later changed their name to the Fourmost. They were different from the others, they did impressions and were very funny, plus good singers as you can hear on their hit records.

When they wanted new stage suits, they asked me for help. They came to Manchester where they chose material, then I took them to my tailor. People say that don't they, my builder, my decorator etc. He wasn't my tailor, he was the tailor who made suits for me. Two weeks later they came back to pick up their new made-to-measure suits, they were quite excited. The tailor showed them the suits, the look on their faces changed to dismay. Instead of the nice shiny brown with a light slub, they had been made the wrong way - inside out. A dull mucky beige, not nice at all. After the initial impact, they saw the funny side, pardon the pun. They took them anyway, wore them on stage for about three weeks then had them died black. Not bad for four pairs of curtains (See Brian Epstein's birthday). Before they went back to Liverpool that day, I took them to the Ko-inoor, which was the first Indian restaurant in Manchester. It was on Oxford Street.

It was very sad when Mike Millward guitar player and great singer died, he had cancer. Years later, Brian O'Hara, who had been the singer and lead guitarist, committed suicide. Not very nice. Billy Hatton, the bass player, I am still friendly with. He and drummer Dave Lovelady carried on in cabaret with Joey Bowers, who was also once a 4Jay.

AFTER HEARING

JOE BROWN's

HIT RECORD

"Picture of you"

see him in person
with his 'BRUVVERS'

AT THE

CAMBRIDGE HALL
SOUTHPORT

SUPPORTED BY THE NORTH'S GREATEST SOUND

the sensational 'BEATLES

PLUS

GERRY AND THE PACEMAKERS

THE BIG THREE

Pete McLaine AND THE DAKOTAS

the 4 JAYS

26 JULY 1962

Watch local press, for details!

Clubs

There was one club we had to play but we really didn't want to. This was the 99 Club in Barrow in Furness. It was too far away - hard to get to. It was a bad "load", a late finish then the load out usually in the rain and then the tedious drive home. Once back in Manchester we'd go to late night Indian restaurants. The Ashad, The Piccadilly and I'm sure there was one called "The Carzy". If we were really desperate we'd go to the Plaza Cafe on Upper Brook Street. This was run by an African guy called Charlie. He would serve up such dishes like "Suicide" and "Asbestos", along with more rice than you could possibly eat. All this on plastic table cloths, it was not my favourite eating place. Everybody else seemed to love it, mind you it was very cheap. Nobby Carr, Manchester character, purveyor of "adult literature" in the '60s and drinking partner of George Best, was an authority on the Plaza Cafe. He would take all sorts of people there and end up with a free meal, good old Nobby, he tells great stories. He is still a friend and is now known as the "Grim Rapper".

Nobby Carr "The Grim Rapper"

World Cup 2010

England, oh my England,
There's a pain in my heart today,
A game we created all those years ago,
Is now just slipping away.

On the anniversary of the battle of Waterloo,
We played a bright American side,
Sad faces no skill or passion,
Without the spirit of Wellington, we dented English pride.

We thought the team would get better,
When the players got things off their chest,
With a slightly better performance,
Could we be as good as the rest.

Against the Germans we prayed with hope, and for glory,
That the team would hear a nations call,
With a goal that was not, getting beat 4-1,
Proved we're actually no good at all.

Washing

Tumble dryers are OK,
They will dry your washing fine,
But they can't compete,
With the smell of your sheets,
When it's been hanging on the line.

The Robin

There's a Robin in our garden,
Surveying it's domain,
A tough little bird the Robin,
Maybe we should be the same.

As you know it's our national feathered friend,
Of the land of "Hope and Glory"
The Robin carries on the same,
But ours is a different story.

Back of Taxi 2006

Early one morning, about 05.15, Helen and I were in a taxi on the way
to Manchester Airport, going for a city break to Barcelona. I was sat
behind the driver, it was still dark. He said "did you see the Beatles on
TV last night." Helen said "no we went to bed early". He went on to
tell us that the Beatles had played in Stockport in the sixties, and how
good all the groups were, including me, back then. Then he tells us that
he goes to the Bull's Head to watch Pete Maclaine & the Clan some
Wednesday nights, and how much he enjoys it, just like old times. I'm
sat behind him listening to all this, then he says, "do you know why that
Pete Maclaine never made it". I said "no, why?" He said "because, he
wasn't tall or good looking enough". I said "I agree with you". We
arrived at departures, I get out, take my cap off, he says "I've just been
talking about you". I paid him and told him I'd buy him a pint next time
he's in the Bull's. Nice way to start your holiday, being told you're an
ugly midget. We couldn't stop laughing.

Leaving Harpurhey

It was 1951,
When we left Harpurhey,
South, to a little village called Miles Platting,
Well! What can I say.

To 56 Energy Street,
A two up, two down terraced house,
Across from some prefabs,
To me, just big enough for a mouse.

My new school was Saint Marks,
I joined the Church Lads brigade,
Today I look back on it fondly,
And cherish the impression it made.

When it came to changing schools,
It was Holland Street for me,
It was a shock to my young system,
A place I didn't want to be.

But one thing we did was go swimming,
Islington, an old Victorian plunge,
There were two pools, a cold one for us,
The other, cockroaches and gung.

We were close to Bradford gas works,
Where I got "coke", the cheapest fuel,
It was my job to get the fire going,
That's before I went to school.

I "had" to join the Black hand gang,
Not quite the "Scuttlers"* of years ago,
But battles were arranged on waste ground,
I had lots of stones to throw.

There were some good times on Energy Street,
The girl next door, my spaniel, Laddie,
This Manchester lad growing up ,
Looking back, I was I suppose quite happy.

* The Gangs of Manchester by Andrew Davies

Life For Living

Trees bend, Rainbows end.
Rivers flow, Flowers grow.
Rain soaks, Smoke chokes.
Sun brings life, Stars shine bright.
Moon romantic, Universe gigantic.
Snow flakes, Waves break.
Shoulders cold, Excuses old.
Hearts ache, Thieves take.
Love for giving, Life for living.

Falling Feather

When I caught a falling feather,
I knew an angel must be near,
I would wish for world peace,
And lots and lots of beer.

The Casino Estoril

In 1970, about twelve months after this photograph (Blackpool) was taken, the Clan were booked to play at the prestigious Casino Estoril in Portugal, not too far from Lisbon. We decided that we would all go. Four weeks in the sun. We put all the bags, guitars, amplifier, stage wear, into our Vauxhall Ventura, it was a big saloon, which was a good job. Then Sue, Simon, Louise, Nicholas, Dave, John and last myself. We drove down to Southampton and rolled onto the ferry, setting sail for Lisbon. While in the bay of Biscay, in one of the roughest seas, the ships doctor came to our cabin. He was going to remove some stitches from Nicholas's chin, Sue wouldn't let him do it because he was rather drunk. He did it the next day. Finally we were heading up the river Tagus and into the port of Lisbon, the beautiful "City of Squares," with the statue of Jesus, just like the one in Rio, watching over. Once off the ship we found the road west to Estoril, and continued on our adventure.

We had four great weeks at the Casino, backed by a fabulous fifteen piece orchestra. There were dancers, acrobats and Portuguese musicians. We closed the show and took the "bow" on a revolving stage. Apparently the reason we were not invited back was that members of the band didn't wear the same shoes. That's showbiz!

The show over, time to head for home. This time we had to drive up to Santander in northern Spain. We piled our brown bodies into the car and headed to the unknown. We travelled north east through Portugal then over the border into Spain. Bypassing Madrid, over the Sierra de Gata and up to Salamanca where we stayed the night. I remember all of us having a drink in a square full of people, we must have been the only English there, the kids loved it. We slept like logs.

Early next morning we headed for Valladolid through the Basque country, and on to Burgos, having a puncture repaired there. Time getting tight now, we had a ferry to catch. We travelled onto Santander, with a minute to spare - and I mean one minute. We drove onto last place on the ship, it started to pull away from the dock before we all got out of the car.

Once again through the bay of Biscay. It was very rough in the night, a bit scary. We finally sailed into Southampton and drove onto English soil, I must say it felt fantastic.

It was Sunday morning the sun was shining we all felt good. Just one slight dampener, that night the Clan had to work. A treble in fact, the The Gainsbourgh, Domino and finishing at Oceans Eleven. Right back down to earth in one fell swoop.

It makes you think, all the people on these talent shows today, don't know they're born. Good luck to 'em.

Pygmalia

1966 The fashion boom in full swing,
Carnaby street was the in thing,
England on top of the world.

London was leading the field,
As Ray Davies and the Kinks revealed,
We were dedicated followers of fashion.

It was like it came over night,
Mary Quant, there in black and white,
So cool to shop at Biba.

The whole country was catching on,
Everybody wanted to join in the fun,
Nowhere more so than, Manchester.

George Best opened his own boutique,
Tucked away, just off Bridge Street,
Footballers would frequent his shop, Edwardia.

But, Pygmalia was the place to go,
Up a little alley, Back Pool Fold,
Owned by Rose and Graham Nash.

It was one of the favourite places,
The Hollies, The Stones and lots of "faces",
Clobber, deliverd by Jeff Banks in a "roller".

Manchester, always a swinging town,
People would come from miles around,
Even "Besty" himself, wore 'malia hipsters.

Although Pygmalia is no longer,
All around grew bigger and stronger,
Into the great city it is today.

The Coat

I used to see this man,
Walking all over the place,
I recognised him by his walk,
Not from the look on his face.

I knew he wasn't a tramp,
Maybe sheltered accommodation,
Never saw him in an overcoat,
I didn't envy his situation.

I saw him one cold winter's morning,
Hand's in pocket's, freezing to death,
Aimlessly shuffling along,
As if trying to catch his frozen breath.

What could I do for this man?
Surely, I could do something,
Maybe I should get him a coat,
Or would that be insulting.

I thought twice when in a charity shop,
Looking through a rail of coat's,
I saw a green once expensive anorak,
It would cost me, a ten pound note.

I saw him a few day's later,
Drove past him and stopped the car,
With the coat on my arm I went up to him,
I asked, are you going far.

I must admit, he looked at me rather funny,
A suspicious look on his face,
Quite understandable really,
This stranger invading his space.

I said, it's cold would you like this coat?
I lied, it's too big for me,
With thanks, he put it on with caution,
Now warmer, my mission complete.

Over year's I still see him,
I assure you, not one to gloat,
But, on cold winter morning's,
He always, wear's the "coat".

Thank You

Graham Nash said "Teach Your Children",
I caught his words when they fell,
Not only do I love my children,
But, I like them as well.

John Lennon and Paul McCartney,
Changed the music world,
Mr Dylan and Mr Cohen,
Thanks for the diamonds and pearls.

Hank Williams, Johnny Cash by his side,
With Elvis, a trio of "kings",
We all knew they would never die,
Music, the greatest thing.

L to R: Me, Jackson Browne, Graham Nash, David Crosby

MTS
ODYSSEUS
1993

Above, with the band on the cruise ship Odysseus 1993.
Below, with the Manhatten's at Butlins during 1965, a month before
I took them to record "You've got your troubles (and I've got mine)".
It was a massive hit for the Fortunes, jam side down again. After
touring for a few months, I wanted to stay in Manchester so I got local
musicians. I wasn't very nice with them, I'm sorry.

When my little girl is smiling...

Not just Rock 'n' Roll

It's not just rock 'n' roll,
From me and the boys in the band,
It's the people who come to see us,
Even lend a helping hand.

Eight years at the Boars Head,
Those crazy Thursday nights,
Then sixteen years at the Bull,
And those scary heart frights.

You came in clammy hot times,
But mostly cold and rain,
Looked up to rock 'n' roll heaven,
Will it ever be the same.

So to say thank you to all those people,
You make it all worthwhile,
And you know for you,
We will go that extra mile.

KEEP ROCKIN'.

MORRISSEY'S MANCHESTER
THE ESSENTIAL SMITHS TOUR
BY PHILL GATENBY
ISBN: 1901746569 - £8.95 - PAPERBACK - 140 PP

'If you're a Smiths fanatic your memorabilia will hardly be complete without this.'
MANCHESTER EVENING NEWS

*'Gatenby's book is much more than a mere guide. It's sometimes an archaeological
expedition to find the lost soul of a city that's been creatively and politically mutilated by
the rise of the new corporate metropolis.'*
MANCHESTER CIVIC SOCIETY

"Don't get on the plane without it.'
MORRISSEY-TOUR.COM

Lyrically unique, Morrissey saw post-industrial Manchester differently. Where most recognised the derelict remains of a Victorian powerhouse, he saw humour, where others saw post-industrial squalor, he felt the frisson of romance. As a result Manchester became as much a part of The Smiths output as the guitars, drums and vocals. As their fame grew, strangers in far away lands wondered about the location of the 'Cemetry Gates' or the setting of 'Vicar in a Tutu'. Unusually, these places still exist and provide the devotee with places of pilgramage - could Manchester offer anything else?

In the first edition of this guidebook, Phill Gatenby set out three tours covering 20 or more sites that either featured in The Smiths music or were fundamental to their development as a band - from early rehearsal spaces to the scene of their most memorable gigs. Now updated, *Morrissey's Manchester* has added new places to visit, more lyrical references and more background information on one of the world's most influential bands.

However the most fundamental change any reader/visitor will notice are the continual changes to Manchester itself - a city in perpetual flux. Since the first edition venues have either been demolished, refurbished or shorn of their identity - hence the need for an update. Now containing 40 new images, an improved layout, a revised map of the city centre, Morrissey's Manchester has been fully updated.

ORDER THESE BOOKS AND MANY MORE AT
WWW.EMPIRE-UK.COM

THE MANCHESTER
MUSICAL HISTORY TOUR
BY PHILL GATENBY & CRAIG GILL

ISBN: 1901746712 - 9781901746716

£7.95 - PAPERBACK - 160pp

PUBLISHED: 10th FEBRUARY 2011

THE MANCHESTER
MUSICAL HISTORY
TOUR
PHILL GATENBY & CRAIG GILL
Foreword by Pete Mitchell

Since the 1950's onwards, Mancunians have had a passion for creating and following great music. Be it live or via recordings, the city has been a magnet for generations of locals – and in recent years music fans from all over the country and beyond – to enjoy. Whilst cities such as Liverpool and Memphis turned their musical heritage into tourist attractions, Manchester kept looking forward, developing new scenes and tastes.

Yet the 2002 film 'Twenty-Four Hour Party People' was probably the point at which Manchester music fans started to look back at the rich musical history of their city. This coincided with the publication of 'Morrissey's Manchester' by Phill Gatenby and numerous other publications penned by luminaries of the Manchester scene.

Following the success of this guide book dedicated to locations associated with The Smiths, author Phill Gatenby put together several tours featuring other world famous Manchester bands from Buzzcocks via Joy Division to Oasis and Doves as well as the various scenes from Beat to Acid House and even Lo-Fi.

An interesting guide for anyone with an interest in British music, this guide documents the various clubs and venues that have influenced Manchester based musicians over the last 50 years.

ABOUT THE AUTHORS

PHILL GATENBY - first began writing for the Manchester City fanzine 'Blue Print' in 1988 and then his own City fanzine 'This Charming Fan' in 1993. After contributing to various other books and magazines, he wrote *Morrissey's Manchester* – the guide to the city's Smiths & Morrissey landmarks in 2002 - and a London edition, *Panic On The Streets*, in 2007. In 2008 he ghost wrote *Sully* and the follow up in 2010, *Sully – Grafting For England*.

CRAIG GILL - is a musician and DJ. Inspired by other great Manchester acts, Craig joined local band Inspiral Carpets in 1985 aged fourteen and over the next ten years he travelled the world, notching up twelve Top 40 singles and four Top 10 albums. A passion for record collecting later came to fruition in the mid nineties, when the Hacienda and Boardwalk nightclubs were amongst many to offer Craig DJ residencies at their clubs, long before the celebrity DJ phenomena was born. Through playing in bands and DJing he has built up strong and lasting friendships with lots of other Manchester musicians, managers and promoters, whose inside knowledge and stories have been invaluable in helping him track down locations and sites to create music tours and its book companion.